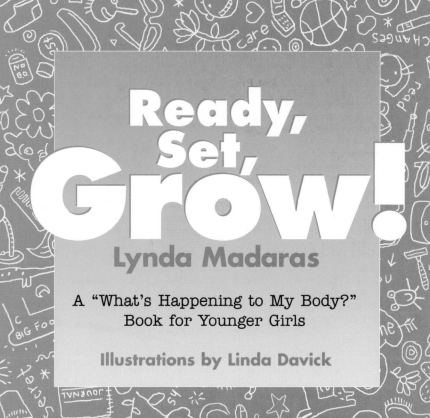

Ready, Set, Grow!

Lynda Madaras

A "What's Happening to My Body?"
Book for Younger Girls

Illustrations by Linda Davick

Newmarket Press ✦ New York

This book is published in the United States of America.

First Edition

10 9 8 7 6 5 4 3 2 1
ISBN 1-55704-565-8 (pb)

10 9 8 7 6 5 4 3 2 1
ISBN 1-55704-587-9 (hc)

Library of Congress Cataloging-in-Publication Data
Madaras, Lynda.
Ready, set, grow! : a what's happening to my body? book for younger girls / Lynda
Madaras ; illustrations by Linda Davick.
        v. cm.
Includes index.
Contents: A note from the author: Hi, I'm Lynda Madaras—What's happening to
me? puberty is about change—Buds, boobs, and bras: your growing breasts—Hair,
there and everywhere: all about body hair—You grow, girl! the height spurt—
Bigger is beautiful: the weight spurt—BO and zits: a survival guide—What's up
down there? a look at your private parts— The inside story: changes you can't
see—That time of the month: all about getting your period—Yours alone: respecting
and protecting your body.
ISBN 1-55704-565-8 (pbk. : alk. paper)—ISBN 1-55704-587-9 (hardcover : alk.
paper)
1. Girls—Growth—Juvenile literature. 2. Girls—Physiology—Juvenile literature. 3.
Puberty—Juvenile literature. [1. Puberty.] I. Davick, Linda, ill. II. Title.
RJ144.M295 2003
612.6'61'08352—dc21
                                           2003009489

QUANTITY PURCHASES

Companies, professional groups, clubs, and other organizations may qualify for
special terms when ordering quantities of this title. For information, write Special
Sales Department, Newmarket Press, 18 East 48th Street, New York, NY 10017;
call (212) 832-3575; (800) 669-3903; fax (212) 832-3629;
or e-mail mailbox@newmarketpress.com.

www.newmarketpress.com

www.whatshappeningtomybody.com

Designed by Linda Davick

Manufactured in the United States of America

*for Peg
and
Olivia*

5

contents

My name is Lynda Madaras.

I write books about growing up and going through puberty. I also teach puberty classes and workshops.

(Chances are, you already know what puberty is. But in case you don't, we'll give you a quick idea. Puberty is a time of changing. It lasts only a few years. But during this time your body changes from a child's body into a woman's body.)

I wrote my first puberty book with my daughter, Area. (It's called The "What's Happening to My Body?" Book for Girls.) Area was going through puberty at the time. She gave me the girl's point of view. She reminded me how it felt to go through puberty. She knew the questions girls wanted answered.

I liked working with Area. She liked working with me, too. (For one thing, she got to correct me all the time.) We went on to write other books about puberty. We wrote My Body, My Self for Girls. It's a workbook. It has quizzes, games, and fun things for girls going through puberty.

(You'll find a list of all our books at the back of this book.)

We had a lot of fun after our books came out. We got to travel around the country. Reporters interviewed us. We got our pictures in the paper. We went on TV and radio shows. We even got to be on *Oprah*! We felt like famous people...for a little while, anyway!

Quite a few years have gone by since that first book. Area got through puberty. She grew up, went to college, and got a job. She fell in love. She got married. And, right now, she's pregnant. As I sit writing this, I am waiting for the phone to ring. I am waiting for the call telling me to come to the hospital. "Come and see your granddaughter get born." I am very excited. I can't wait to say, "Hello, baby, welcome to the earth."

It's not just Area that's changed during these years. Believe it or not, puberty has also changed. Well, of course, what happens hasn't changed. But *when* it happens has.

Today puberty is happening to younger

girls. When Area and I wrote our first book, most girls were in the sixth grade or higher before they started. Now, the first signs of puberty often happen to a girl in the third or fourth grade. (Sometimes even earlier!) So I've written this book for girls of all ages. I think younger girls will like it. But it's not just for younger girls. It is written for all of you who are thinking about or going through puberty.

As I said, Area got through puberty and went on to other things. Not me! I've stayed with puberty. I've written and taught and spoken about it. I have talked to girls all across the country. I've also gotten zillions of letters from girls who've read my books.

Most girls don't hold back. They tell me just what they're thinking. They ask questions. Many of the things they say are here in this book. Many of their questions are here, too, along with my answers. So girls like you helped to write this book.

I hope you like the book. I hope it helps you understand and enjoy your changing body. And I hope one day my granddaughter reads it and it helps her, too.

one

What's Happening to Me?

Puberty Is about Change

You're growing up. Of course, that's nothing new. After all, you've been growing up all your life.

Ever since the day you were born, you've been growing in many ways. Year by year, you've been growing bigger. You've been getting taller and heavier. But this growing up is different.

Maybe you've noticed little bumps growing under your nipples. Your chest is not flat anymore. Sometimes the little bumps may feel itchy or sore. You are growing breasts!

Or maybe you're seeing some hairs in places that were bare before. Hair may be growing on your "private parts." (This hair is called pubic hair.) Hair may be starting to grow under your arms, too.

Has any of this stuff happened to you? If so, you may be asking, "Am I weird?"

No! You are not weird. You are 100% NORMAL! You're just starting puberty.

What if none of this has happened to you yet? Does *that* mean you're weird?

No! You are not weird, either. You are 100% NORMAL, too! You haven't started puberty yet, but you will. Sooner or later all of us start puberty.

What Is Puberty?
Puberty is a special time in a girl's life. During puberty, a girl's body changes into a woman's body. This doesn't happen all at once. It takes

14

List of Changes

Get breasts

Pubic hair

Growing really fast

More body fat

Hips wider

Hair under your arms

Darker hair
on arms and legs

Start shaving legs
(maybe)

Sweat more

Body odor changes

Zits, pimples, acne

Discharge

Get your period

Get cramps

Changes in your
private parts

Ovulate

Female organs mature

years to go through puberty. From start to finish, puberty may take anywhere from two to five (or more) years.

How does puberty start? What happens first? That depends. For many girls, the first sign of puberty is their breasts starting to develop. But for many others, puberty starts with the growth of some pubic hair. Less often, under-arm hair is the first change.

The first changes are just the start. They are followed by many others. Maybe you already know about these changes. In my puberty classes, we make lists of these changes. I divide everyone into teams. Each team has an outline of the female body. They also have a bunch of markers.

On your mark, get set, go! Each team writes as many changes as they can. Then, I call time. The team with the longest list wins. At the left is one winning team's list.

You may not know what some of the words in this list mean. Not to worry! This book will teach you about all these changes.

As you can see, puberty is a time of many changes. The kids in my classes have lots of questions about these changes. Chances are, you do, too. That's what this book is all about—answering your questions about growing up.

When Does Puberty Start?

Girls don't all start puberty at the same age. Most girls start between the ages of eight and a half and 11. But some start puberty earlier than eight and a half. And some start later than 11. Each girl is special. Each girl's body grows at the rate that is just right for her.

It's hard to be different. Girls who are late starters often wish puberty would start sooner.

I wish I was further along. It seems like I'm the last in my class to get boobs.

Girls who are early starters often wish puberty had started later.

I didn't want to start before my friends. I didn't like being different from my friends.

If you're an early or a late starter, try to be patient. Know that your body is growing up at the speed that's right for you. In a few years, you and your friends will all have started puberty. Then it won't matter who was first or

last. After all, we all end up in the same place—grown up!

Feelings about Puberty and Growing Up

I just started puberty and I'm really proud. I'm really excited and happy about it.

When I started to get breasts I didn't want people to see them. I used to wear baggy shirts so they wouldn't show.

Puberty is scary. Sometimes I think about all these changes and it's, well, kind of scary.

You may feel really proud about starting puberty. Or you may feel embarrassed. You may be a little scared thinking about all the changes. You may feel one way one time, and another way another time. Feelings are like that.

When you're feeling proud, enjoy that feeling. Hold your head high. If you have some scary or embarrassed feelings, take heart. You're not alone! Other girls are feeling the same way. We all go through the same changes. We all make it!

For most of us, puberty is a mixed bag. Sometimes you'll feel great. Other times, you

Growing Up Doesn't Mean You're a Grown-Up

When puberty starts you might think that now you have to act differently.

"I'm afraid that now I'll have to always act grown up. But I don't want to have to act all grown up."

You may feel this way, too. But puberty doesn't happen all at once. True, you are growing up. But that doesn't mean you have to be a grown-up. You've got lots of time yet. Your body may be changing, but you can still be a kid. You can still climb a tree.

You can still be

"just friends" with boys. You can act goofy. You can still play "little girl" games.

You can be grown up for a time. Then you can act like a kid again. You can watch cartoons one day and MTV the next.

You can do whatever you feel like doing. It's up to you. Be what you want to be.

may not feel so great. That's part of growing up.

Fact is, puberty isn't always a piece of cake. But there are things you can do to make it a little easier. Be prepared. Read this book with your mom, dad, or another adult you trust. Ask questions. Get the facts. Know what's happening to your body. Puberty is a lot less scary when you know what to expect.

You can also read this book with your friends. Talk about puberty changes. Giggle. Ask how your friends feel about their changing bodies. Talk about how you feel.

The more you know and the more you talk about your feelings, the easier it will be!

Be what you want to be.

two

Buds, Boobs, and Bras
Your Growing Breasts

I kept wanting to grow up. Then my breasts started to grow! I thought, "Finally, it's happening."

I was so happy when my breasts started growing...I was so proud. I felt real grown up.

I didn't look forward to getting boobs. Once I had them, I didn't want them. It was embarrassing when boys "looked" at me.

When I saw my boobs were developing...well, I just wasn't ready for it. I thought, "This can't be happening. Not yet!" I wasn't ready for the whole "Becoming-a-Woman" bit.

You may be happy about your breasts starting to grow. Or you may not be happy at all. Either way, sooner or later, your breasts will begin to grow.

Breast Growth Begins
Breast growth starts with breast buds. These are little bumps that form under your nipples. A breast bud is flat and round, like a button. It makes your nipple and the ring of tissue around it stick out from your chest.

At least I don't have eight!

A bud may develop under one nipple before the other. Don't worry. Before too long, the other breast bud will begin to grow.

Your breast buds may be itchy or sore. At times, they may be *really* sore! Not to worry! It's perfectly normal.

For many girls, breast buds are the first sign of puberty. Most girls get breast buds when they are between the

When I saw my boobs were developing... well, I just wasn't ready for it.

ages of eight and a half and 11. But everyone is different. Some girls are only seven when their breasts begin to develop. And that's OK. Others don't get breast buds until they are 12 or older. And that's OK, too.

Nipples, Too

At the same time you develop breast buds, you may notice other changes. The ring around each nipple, the areola, gets larger and darker in color. Later, the nipple itself will also get larger.

> **Areola (ah-REE-oh-luh):** The ring of skin around the nipple that gets bigger and darker during puberty

Nipples come in all shapes, sizes, and colors. They're often very sensitive to touch. When cold, they may get hard and stick out.

Sometimes, instead of sticking out, a nipple will point inward. It's kind of like belly buttons. There are "innies" and "outies." Most nipples are "outies." But a girl may have one or both nipples pointing inward. As the breasts develop, an "innie" may turn into an "outie," or it may not. It's OK if you have "innies" or "outies"—or even one of each!

Breast Stages

Breast buds are just the beginning. Your breasts keep on growing and changing during puberty.

21

Doctors talk about five stages of breast growth. Look at the pictures on this page. Can you tell which stage you're in?

Stage 1 Childhood
Breast buds have not started to grow. The chest is almost flat. Only the nipples stick out from the chest.

Stage 2 Breast Buds
The breasts start to develop. Breast buds form under the nipples. The nipple and its ring stand out from the chest. The ring gets bigger and darker in color. The nipple, too, may get bigger and change color.

Stage 3 Still Growing
The nipple and its ring grow larger. The breast itself also begins to get bigger.

Stage 4 Nipple and Ring Puff Up
The ring around the nipple "puffs up." The nipple and its ring get darker and start to "stick out" more. They form their own little mound on the breast. Some girls skip this stage.

Stage 5 Adult
The ring around the nipple isn't puffed up

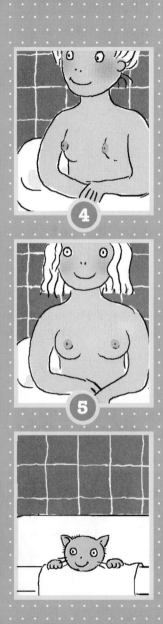

any more. The nipple and its ring no longer stick up as a separate mound. The breasts reach their adult size, or close to it. (Even after you reach this stage, your breasts may grow a bit larger. They may keep growing until you reach your early 20s. They may also get bigger if you have a baby.)

Most girls take three or four years to go from breast buds to adult breasts. But we're not all the same. Some girls only take two years. Others take five years or more.

When you start to develop has nothing to do with *how fast* you get to Stage 5. Also, *when* you start has nothing to do with *how big* your breasts will end up.

Size and Shape

Breasts come in all sizes and shapes. Some are big. Some are small. Some are pointy. Some are more rounded. Some hang low, others sit up high. All are perfectly fine!

Breasts are a big deal in our culture. People pay a lot of attention to them. All the time, we see women with big, full breasts on TV and in the movies. So it may seem like that's how everyone's are supposed to look.

It's no wonder some girls worry about how their breasts look. Some wish they had bigger breasts.

Have you seen magazine ads that promise to make your breasts bigger? Don't believe these ads. These creams and other products don't work. Gadgets to "exercise" the breasts won't make them bigger. There's no way that a cream or "exercise" can make your breasts larger.

All the time, we see women with big, full breasts on TV and in the movies. So it may seem like that's how everyone's are supposed to look.

Many girls with large breasts are unhappy, too. They get tired of stares and comments. And very large breasts can cause back pain.

Too many girls think there's something not right about their breasts. They couldn't be more wrong. Do you worry about the size or shape of your breasts? Don't! Your breasts, big or small, will look just perfect on you.

Bras
When should a girl start wearing a bra? Does

she even need to wear a bra at all?

There are no set answers to these questions. You decide for yourself. Some girls wear a bra for comfort. They like the support a bra gives. It keeps their breasts from "jiggling." Some girls play sports. They need a bra to protect their breasts from injury.

What about wearing a bra even if you don't really "need" one? Sure, why not?

Some girls wear a bra because they feel funny without one. They don't like their nipples showing through a thin shirt. Many girls wear tank tops or undershirts instead of bras. Some girls don't like bras and just won't wear one. And that's fine, too.

What about wearing a bra even if you don't really "need" one? Sure, why not? Lots of girls do. There are bras to fit every size, even if you have very small breasts.

What if you want a bra, but are too embarrassed to ask for one? Our advice: Ask anyhow. Your parents may be waiting for you to bring up the topic. They might not be asking because they're afraid they'd embarrass you!

Many girls want help when they buy their first bra. A good friend or an older sister could help. And don't forget mom or even dad.

My First Bra

"I remember when I got my first bra. It was really freaky. A boy was in the next aisle. I didn't want him to see me buying a bra. My mom helped me out. She said, 'Go look at the shoes. I'll get the bra.'"

● ● ● ● ● ● ● ● ● ● ●

"I got my first bra last year. I was living with my dad then. I was sooo embarrassed. Finally I said, 'Dad, I need a bra.' He said, 'I don't know a whole lot about it. But what are they gonna do? Kick us out of the store?' He talked to the lady at the store and just handled it all. He was real cool."

Bra Sizes

Bras come in sizes like 28AAA, 30AA 32B, 34C, 36B, 38D. No, these aren't the answers to a math quiz. They really are bra sizes. But what in the world is a size 28AAA, 34B, or 38D? How do you know what size is right for you?

No sweat—we'll help you with it. Just remember this. Bra sizes have two parts: the number part and the letter part. The number part is band size. It tells how big around the bra is when it's fastened. The letter, or letters, is the cup size. It tells how much room the cup has.

AAA is the smallest cup size. Next comes AA. These cup sizes are for girls who are just starting to develop. Girls who are a little more developed take an A or a B cup. Grown women often take a C cup. Those with larger breasts will need a D cup or larger.

The band size is usually a number between 28 and 38 inches. You might want to measure your band size before you go shopping for a bra. It's easy to do. You measure around your ribs just below your breasts. This is your rib size. Now look in the chart to find your band size.

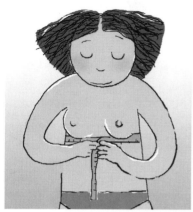

Measure the band size.

Rib Size	Band Size
22-23 inches	28
24-25 inches	30
26-27 inches	32
28-29 inches	34
30-31 inches	36
32-33 inches	38

Measure the cup size.

To get an idea of your cup size, you need to measure again. This time measure across the fullest part of your breast. Compare the result with the your rib size. Are they the same? Then, try an AA cup. Is the result 1 inch more than your rib size? Try an A cup. If it's 2 inches bigger, try a B. If it's 3 inches bigger, try a C cup…and so on. But don't go by this alone. Always try different sizes before you buy.

Bra Choices

Breasts come in all shapes and sizes. Bras do, too. There are many styles and types to choose from. Before you buy, try different bras. Also, try the same bra in different sizes.

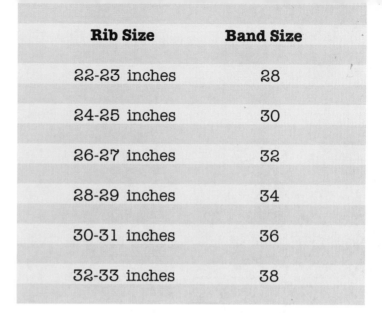

One-size-fits-all bras are made of stretchy material. They are very comfortable. They're good for girls who don't need a lot of support but want to wear a bra.

Training bras don't train your breasts to grow. They're just bras with AAA or AA cups for girls with smaller breasts.

Underwire bras have wires sewn in the edges of the cups. They give extra support. They are a good choice if you wear a C or larger cup.

Soft cup bras don't have wires. They don't give as much support as a wire bra. They are a good choice for a B cup or smaller.

Padded bras have padding inside the cup. They make your breasts look larger.

Push-up bras have padding, too. They push your breasts together and up. They also make your breasts look larger.

Sports bras look like cut-off tank tops. They keep your breasts from bouncing when you run or play. Some girls love their sports bras. They wear them even when they're not playing sports because they're so comfortable.

I am 14 and wear a 34A bra. My sister is younger than I am and already she wears a C cup. I don't want to have small breasts when I'm all grown up. How can I help but feel bad?

There's still plenty of time for your breasts to grow. But even if they don't, there is no reason to feel bad.

Chances are you feel bad because you think others won't find you attractive. But what's attractive is not the same for everyone.

In the 1920s, the "in" look was super thin, with almost no breasts. Today big breasts are in fashion. Tomorrow? Who knows? Maybe three-breasted women will be "in."

Fashions change. But one thing is always true. Breasts, small or large, are beautiful. So know that your breasts are just right for you. Enjoy being beautiful.

Both of my breasts started growing at the same time. But now one is a lot bigger than the other one. Will I grow up all lopsided?

One breast may develop a little faster than the other. Don't worry. The other breast will most likely catch up. If it doesn't catch up all the way, that's OK. It's normal to have breasts that are not exactly the same size.

Q **I'm 12. I'm just now starting to get breast buds. Why am I so slow?**

A Some girls start to develop breasts sooner than others. But sooner or later, every girl goes through the stages of breast development. Your breasts will develop at the age that is just right for you. Your body is special. Be proud of your body as it is right now.

Q **I've developed really quickly. I have bigger breasts than the other girls in my class. Now some of my girl friends are acting weird. What can I do?**

A There's not much you can do about the size of your breasts. But you might try telling your friends something like this: "Look, we all go through puberty. I'm a little ahead right now. But in the end, you'll catch up, and we'll all have fully grown breasts."

Q **I have big breasts for my age. Kids at school tease me. Now I'm just the girl with the boobs. Nothing else about me seems to matter. What can I do?**

A This kind of teasing can be very hurtful. It affects how you feel about yourself and your changing body. Kids may act like it's all just "good fun." But it's not fun for you. You don't have to put up with it.

Tell these kids that you want it to stop. Be clear with them about what is not OK. If that doesn't work, ask your parents, a teacher, or a counselor to help you stop it. To learn more about dealing with this problem, see pages 118-120.

three

Hair, There and Everywhere
All about Body Hair

Puberty is a hairy time! You sprout new hairs here and there. Places that were bare before suddenly have hair. All at once, you're a hairier you!

Now don't get me wrong. I'm not saying you will turn into Werewolf Girl overnight. But during puberty you do grow new hair on certain parts of your body. This chapter will tell you where and when to expect this new hair.

Pubic Hair

I was taking a bath and, Oh wow! I saw a pubic hair. I got excited and read a lot of books.

You've never had any hair there before. It looks funny. All of a sudden there's hair where there never was any. It just looks...not right. I guess you get used to it.

I just wasn't ready. I remember when I first saw my pubic hairs growing. I thought, oh no. I don't want this to start happening to me yet.

Grown women have a triangle of short, curly hair growing in the area between their legs. It's called pubic hair. Some women have a lot of pubic hair. Others don't have so much. Pubic hair may be red, black, brown, or blond. It may not be the same color as the hair on your head. When you are old, it may turn gray.

During puberty, girls begin to grow their first pubic hairs. These first hairs are more straight than curly. They may not have much color.

Now don't get me wrong. I'm not saying you will turn into Werewolf Girl overnight.

There aren't many of them. You may have to look very closely to see them.

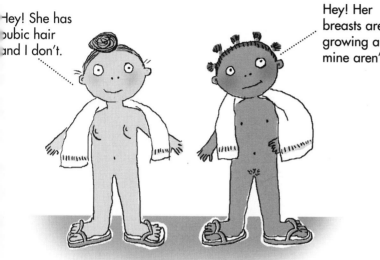

Hey! She has pubic hair and I don't.

Hey! Her breasts are growing and mine aren't.

Some girls start growing pubic hair before they get breast buds. For other girls, pubic hair only starts to grow after their breasts start to develop.

Some girls start growing pubic hair before they get breast buds. For them, pubic hair may be the first sign of puberty. For other girls, pubic hair only starts to grow after their breasts start to develop. And some girls develop breast buds and pubic hair at about the same time.

Pubic Hair Stages

The first few pubic hairs are just the start. You grow more as puberty continues. As with breasts, there are five stages of pubic hair growth. Look at the pictures on the next page. Can you tell which stage you're in?

Stage 1 Childhood

You may notice fine, short hair that grows on the belly and other places. But there is no pubic hair.

Stage 2 First Pubic Hairs

The first pubic hairs begin to grow. There aren't very many of them. Most girls get their first pubic hairs when they're eight and a half to 11. But it can happen earlier or later than this.

Stage 3 Still Growing

The pubic hairs are curly and darker. There are more of them.

Stage 4 Hair More Curly and Wiry

There is more pubic hair than in Stage 3. The hairs are as dark, curly, and wiry as they will be in the adult stage. They form a triangle. But they don't cover as wide an area as they will in Stage 5.

Stage 5 Adult

The pubic hair forms a bushy triangle. It reaches to the edge of the thighs. In some women, it grows out onto the thighs. It may also grow up toward the belly button.

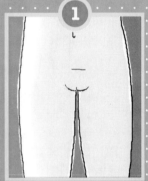

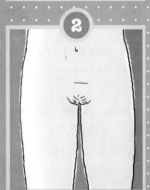

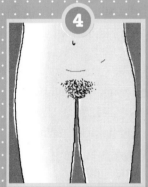

Your stage of pubic hair growth may not be the same as your stage of breast growth. The two things don't always go hand in hand. You could be in Breast Stage 3, but only in Pubic Hair Stage 2. Or, you might be in Pubic Hair Stage 4, but only in Breast Stage 2. Don't worry if your breast and pubic hair stages don't match. It's perfectly normal!

Underarm and Body Hair

During puberty, hair also starts to grow in your armpits. For a few girls, underarm hair is the very first sign of puberty. They grow underarm hair even before they grow pubic hair or breast buds.

For most girls, underarm hair starts to grow a year or so after the first pubic hairs. But some girls are near the end of puberty before they get any underarm hair.

The hair on your arms and legs changes during puberty, too. Before puberty, this hair is soft and fine. It doesn't have much color. During puberty, it gets thicker. It also gets darker. It may seem like there's more of it.

Shaving Legs and Underarms

Should you shave your leg and underarm hair? It's up to you. (And, of course, your

A Hairy Situation

"I was young when I started shaving my legs. I thought I was the only girl with hair on her legs. Now I know that wasn't true. Many girls were as hairy as I was. Some were hairier. But I was too worried about myself to see this."

"Girls have to shave their legs and under their arms, but guys don't. This stinks! Why should we have to when they don't have to?"

"I shave my legs. I like the way it feels after I'm done. Besides, it looks a lot better than having hair all over my legs."

"All of my friends shave their legs. They start talking about it. I just try and change the

parents. You'll need their OK before you start shaving.) Just remember: Once you start, you have to shave often to stay smooth.

Besides shaving, there are other ways to remove hair. There are waxes and creams. But creams can irritate the skin. Waxing can hurt. A doctor can zap the hair with a laser. There are machines that burn the hair root. But these methods cost a lot. And they must be done by a person who is trained in their use. Shaving is the safest and easiest way to get rid of underarm and leg hair.

There are different kinds of razors. Most girls use plastic, throw-away razors. You just throw the whole razor away when the blade gets dull. Many girls like refillable razors. With these, you replace only the blade and its holder or just the blade itself.

Shaving is safe, but it's easy to cut yourself. The blades can also scrape the skin and cause "razor burn." This is a painful, red rash. A dull razor blade can pull, or drag, on the skin, causing razor burn. Here are a few tips to help you shave safely.

Be careful. Go slowly and go easy. Don't mash or grind the razor into your skin. Don't go over the same spot again and again.

On your legs, shave upward in long, even strokes. Under your arms, use short strokes. Shave in the direction of hair growth.

Make sure your blade is clean, sharp, and free of nicks. Rinse the hair from your blade often. Clean your razor well when you're done. Dropping a razor can cause nicks you can't see. If you drop it, change to a new blade. Blades may get dull after four to five shaves. Change them often.

You want the blade to slide smoothly over your skin. Use warm water to wet the hair first. This softens the hair and cuts down on razor drag. Give the water a few minutes to work. Then use a shaving cream or gel. Plain soap will do in a pinch, but it can dull blades.

After shaving, rinse with cool water. Then pat (don't rub) your skin dry. Your skin is very sensitive after shaving. Wait half an hour before putting creams or lotions on your legs or going swimming. Wait several hours before using an underarm deodorant.

Never lend or borrow a razor. This can spread germs.

topic. I don't shave my legs yet and don't want to. But it feels like shaving is something you 'have to' do."

"I think girls only shave to please someone else. They get pressured into it. Or they are brainwashed by all the ads with smooth, hairless women. They are just following society's rules. I don't shave and I'm not about to start."

"I shave my legs and armpits. But I don't do it because someone says I have to. I do it for myself. I like the smooth feeling I get."

Q&A

Q **I saw three dark hairs down there. It looked gross. I didn't want them. I didn't know about pubic hairs then. I pulled them out with tweezers. Was it wrong to pull them out?**

A No. But your pubic hairs will just grow back. And, ouch! Plucking hairs can hurt. There's also a small chance of getting an infection. The best advice: Let them grow.

Q **I don't have much pubic hair. It's been growing for three years. Shouldn't I have a lot of pubic hair by now? Is it because I'm Asian?**

A It's likely that you will grow more pubic hair before you are an adult. But we are not all the same. Some women do have more pubic hair than others. The amount depends partly on race and ethnic background. Some Asian women do have less pubic hair than women from other backgrounds.

Q **My pubic hair grew in kind of quick. The other morning I found some pubic hairs in my panties. Is it all going to fall out now?**

A No. Hair on all parts of the body is always being lost. Then new hairs grow to replace them. Think about the hairs on your head.

You can lose a few of them. But that doesn't mean you are going bald.

Q When a girl shaves her legs, does she just go up to her knees? Or does she shave her thighs, too?

A It's up to her. Some girls don't like the way hair looks on their thighs. They always shave above their knees. Others don't shave there because the hair on their thighs is soft and light. Some only shave in the summer. They don't want hair to show when they wear shorts or swimsuits.

Q I have a few black hairs around my nipples. Is this weird, or what? It's not a lot of hair. I cut them off. Is that OK? What should I do about them?

A It's not weird. It's perfectly normal. All women have some hair around their breasts. The hairs are usually light and soft. Sometimes a few dark and stiff hairs grow there. Often these dark hairs first show up during puberty.

There's no need to remove them. They will just grow back. It's OK to trim them with scissors. Some women shave these hairs. But be careful! The skin around your nipple is very sensitive. Never use waxes or cream hair removers on breast hairs.

Some women use tweezers to pull out these hairs. But that can hurt. Here again, there's a small chance of infection. The best bet: Let them be. They're perfectly normal!

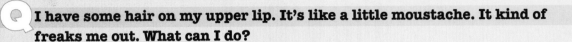

Q I have some hair on my upper lip. It's like a little moustache. It kind of freaks me out. What can I do?

A Many girls have some hair on the upper lip. This is totally normal. (Sometimes, but not often, a lot of hair may suddenly appear on a girl's face. If this happens to you, see your doctor.)

You can find products for dealing with unwanted hair at any drug-store. There are facial hair bleaches. They lighten the hairs, making them harder to see. There are facial hair remover creams that dissolve hair. There are also waxing kits for removing facial hair. You spread the wax over the hair. Then you pull the wax off. The hairs, stuck in the wax, are also pulled off. These products get rid of the hair for a while, but it will grow back. Talk to your mom or dad before using them. Your parent can help you to follow all the directions correctly.

And think carefully before you do anything. Once you start, you will have to keep doing it on a regular basis. So wait a bit before doing anything. These hairs may not be as noticeable after a while.

four

You Grow, Girl!
The Height Spurt

Puberty is a time when we grow up...and up...and up! Of course, we grow taller all during childhood. But we grow much faster during puberty. This time of really fast growth is called the height spurt.

I grew six inches last year! At first, I didn't really notice. Then it was like, wow, overnight! One morning I woke up and the ground just seemed really far away...way down there.

Most girls don't grow six inches in one year. And it never happens overnight. But all of us do go through a height spurt during puberty.

The Height Spurt

Most children grow about two inches a year. Once the height spurt begins, growth speeds up. A girl may grow four inches a year. That's twice as fast!

The height spurt lasts a few years. Then growth slows back down. Most girls add around nine inches during their height spurts. But we aren't all the same. You may grow more or less than this.

Boys go through a height spurt, too. For girls, the height spurt happens early in puberty. For boys, it comes later. In fact, boys usually start their height spurts about two years later than girls do. But the height spurt lasts longer in boys than it does in girls.

Most girls start their height spurts around the age of ten. Most boys don't start before the

Most girls start their height spurts around the age of ten. Most boys don't start before the age of 12. That's why 11- and 12-year-old girls are often taller than boys their age.

age of 12. That's why 11- and 12-year-old girls are often taller than boys their age. Then boys start their growth spurt. Most of them soon catch up to and pass the girls.

Feet First

During the height spurt, all your bones grow. But some bones start their growth spurt before others. Guess which bones start first?

You guessed it! It's the bones in your feet. Your feet can be almost full-grown early in the height spurt.

I remember when I was ten or 11. My feet were growing really fast. I needed three pairs of shoes in one school year! I didn't know what was happening. Maybe my feet were just going to keep on getting bigger and bigger.

When their feet grow quickly, some girls worry. They think they'll end up with giant feet! But there's no need to worry. Your feet won't keep on growing so quickly. They will slow down while the rest of your body keeps growing. Soon your body catches up with your feet.

Too Tall? Too Short?

Some girls are unhappy about their height.

They feel they are "too tall" or "too short." Being different from the other kids isn't always easy.

I'm really tall. I hate being such a giant. Clothes in the store don't fit. People call me "beanpole" and "stick." They say really stupid things to me. I wish I was shorter, like my friends.

I don't like being tall and skinny. Clothes are hard to find. Pants are a pain in the butt and that's no joke. I never get to dress up in heels. I'd just tower over everyone. People stare at you in the mall. You're taller than all the guys.

Do you think you're too tall? Does it help to know there are lots of tall models and women sports stars? Once upon a time, they may have thought they were too tall. Now they love being tall! Keep your chin up. You may grow to love your height. Here's what some older girls had to say about being tall.

When their feet grow quickly, some girls worry. They think they'll end up with giant feet!

I'm tall and proud of it. I wish I could be one inch taller. Then I'd be an even six feet tall. I'm taller than most of my friends...I feel like I'm this Superwoman, Amazon queen.

I'm five feet ten inches tall. I just act like it's not a problem and that's how other people take it, too. I date guys who are shorter, taller, the same height as I am. It just doesn't matter what your height is.

Other girls find it hard to be short.

I'm just about the smallest girl in my class. Some of the guys from the basketball team make a joke of me. They pick me up, tuck me under one arm, and run down the hall with me. It's like I'm a toy, not a person.

I am four feet ten. I'm always wishing I was taller. People think I'm a little kid. They pat me on the head. They say, "Where's your mama?"

Do you wish you were taller? Fact is, you can't really do much about your height. But what really counts is the way you deal with it. You don't have to be six feet tall to be a good friend. You don't have to be tall to be funny or smart or popular. You can't change your height. But you *can* go out there and be all

How Tall Will I Be?

No one can tell for sure how tall you'll be. But there are some clues.

Here's one clue. Has your height spurt begun? If you're tall before the height spurt, then you're likely to be a tall woman. If you are short as a child, it's likely you'll be a short woman. But it doesn't always work this way. Some girls are short before puberty. Then the spurt kicks in. They end up being among the tallest girls in their class!

Here's another clue. Do you have an older sister? If so, you're ▶

likely to grow at least as tall as she is.

Here's one more clue. Is your dad five or more inches taller than your mom? If so, you will probably grow to be at least as tall as your mother.

Did one clue say you would be tall? Did another say you'd be short? Well, we never said they were perfect! They are only clues, after all.

the things you want to be.

I'm a shortie and kind of all-around small. It's never been a big problem. Most of the time, I don't even think about my height. You get away with a lot being short. People think you're cute. I can buy clothes in the kids' department. I save a lot of money.

I am five feet, and almost out of college. I won't grow anymore. That's fine by me. I love being short. I think it's fun. I don't get upset when somebody jokes about my height. I tell them I'm normal and they're way tall.

Growing Strong Bones

During the height spurt, your bones grow quickly. Your growing bones need lots of calcium. Calcium makes bones strong. Not getting enough can stunt your growth. It can weaken your bones. It can even lead to very serious bone disease when you're older. You must get enough calcium *while your bones are growing.* There's no way to make up for missed calcium later on in your life.

Doctors are worried about girls your age. Many of them are not getting the calcium they need. What will happen to these girls later in life? Will they develop serious bone diseases?

No one knows for sure. But be on the safe side. Make sure you get plenty of calcium now.

Calcium (KAL-see-uhm): A nutrient, found mostly in dairy foods, that helps bones grow strong

How? By getting lots of calcium in your diet and by exercising. Drink milk instead of soda pop. Eat foods that are rich in calcium. Cheese and yogurt are good choices. Calcium is now added to some foods, like low-fat milk and orange juice. Check the labels. Look for the words "fortified with calcium."

You need plenty of exercise, too. Exercise helps put the calcium you eat into your bones. So don't be a couch potato. Get up. Shake a leg and get going. (You'll learn just how much exercise you need in Chapter 5.)

Not getting enough calcium can lead to a very serious bone disease when I'm older.

Be on the safe side.
Make sure you get plenty of calcium now.

Q&A

Q **I started my period a few months ago. I read in a book that you stop growing once you get your period. Is this true?**

A No. Growth has usually slowed by the time of your first period. But you don't stop growing altogether. Most girls grow about two more inches after they get their periods.

Q **I'm ten. Sometimes I have pains in my legs. My mom says they're just growing pains. Is there really such a thing?**

A Yes, growing pains are real...a real pain! They happen most often around the ages of ten or eleven. Growing pains may happen in the legs or in other parts of the body. They can happen in the arms, shoulders, back, and groin. Growing pains come and go. Sooner or later, they go away and don't come back. If it's not a come-and-go kind of pain or if the pain is bad, it should be checked out. You should see a doctor. Talk to your mom or dad about it.

Q **At the end of the year, all the girls in my grade have to go to the nurse's office. We have to get tested for scoliosis. What is it? What's the test like? Does it hurt? Do you have to take your clothes off?**

During puberty a girl's spine grows quickly. Once in a while, this causes the spine to curve in an abnormal way. This problem is called scoliosis (skoh-lee-OH-sis). Very few girls show signs of this problem. The few that do shouldn't panic. Most only need regular checkups to make sure the curve doesn't get worse. Some girls with scoliosis do have to wear a brace for a while. In all cases, it's easiest to deal with the problem when it's found early.

The exam doesn't hurt. The nurse will check that your hips and shoulders are level. The nurse will also look at your back and check the curve of your spine. You may have to take off your shirt. If you wear a bra, you can leave it on.

I'm 12. I'm not the shortest girl in my grade. But I am on the short side. I'm afraid I might not grow any taller. Is there anything I can do to get taller? Could vitamins or a special diet help me?

There's nothing you can do to make yourself taller. But give yourself time. Chances are, you still have some growing ahead of you. Try not to worry too much. Even if you don't get much taller, that's okay, too.

I heard that drinking coffee or tea could stop you from growing any taller. Is this true? What about smoking? I know that smoking is bad for you at any age. But is it worse during puberty? Can it stunt your growth?

Drinking coffee or tea will not stop you from growing. But you do need calcium for your bones. Don't let coffee or tea take the place of low-fat milk or other calcium-rich drinks.

Smoking won't stop you from growing. But smoking is, as you say, "worse during puberty." Your body is working hard to grow so fast. It is less able to cope with the poisons from smoking. That's why young women who smoke are more likely to get breast cancer when they are older.

Q **I'm very tall...really tall. I'm sick of people saying, "How's the weather up there?" or "Why are you so tall?" I hear so many stupid questions. I never know what to say. Some yo-yo says, "Do you play basketball?" What am I supposed to say?**

A You could say, "No, do you play miniature golf?"

It is hard to deal with rude people. It doesn't matter what they are being rude about. You could be polite and answer the rude question. You could ignore it. You could say, "I don't answer rude questions." You could tell them off. People may not mean to be rude. They just don't think before they open their mouths. You might let them know their question isn't nice. There are some people who are rude on purpose. They just have bad manners. They really are not worth worrying about.

five

Bigger Is Beautiful
The Weight Spurt

Puberty is a time when we put on pounds. We add a layer of fat under the skin. The fat rounds out our hips and thighs. This gives us a more curvy, womanly shape. Our bones also grow bigger and heavier. So do our muscles. Our breasts develop. It all adds up, and we have a weight spurt.

The weight spurt is like the height spurt. It is a time of extra-fast growth during puberty. And it happens at about the same time as the height spurt.

The weight spurt lasts a few years. A girl may gain ten or more pounds in just one year. In all, most girls add about forty pounds. Of course, we're not all the same. You may gain more or less than this.

Too Fat?

When the weight spurt hits, some girls freak out. They get on the scale. *"Oh no, another ten pounds! I'm getting fat!"*

Fat pads fill out their hips and thighs. Then they really go nuts. They look in the mirror. All they see is wider hips and thighs. Now they're sure. *"I am way too fat!"*

But these body changes DO NOT mean that you are getting fat. These changes are normal. You're *supposed* to gain weight during puberty.

Dieting Can Be Dangerous

First, girls decide they are too fat. Then, they decide to start dieting. They skip meals or go on a crazy "fad" diet. It seems like there's a new fad diet every week. They all promise

Fact is, many girls your age think they're too fat when they're not. They are perfectly normal. Why do so many girls think they need to diet when they don't?

quick loss of weight. They sound too good to be true. And they are! Fad diets don't provide the variety of foods your body needs to be healthy.

Skipping meals and fad diets almost never work in the long run. You may lose some weight at first. But before too long, you gain it back. You haven't really changed your eating habits. So when you stop dieting, you just gain back all you lost. You may even gain back more than you lost!

Dieting can be very bad for your health. You need to eat a variety of foods. Everyone needs a healthy diet. During puberty, it's extra important that you eat right. Otherwise, your body will not get all the vitamins, minerals, and other good things it needs.

You're having a growth spurt. Your body needs extra energy. You get it from the food you eat. If you do not eat enough of the right kind of foods, it may slow or even stop your growth.

Dieting during puberty can be harmful in other ways, too. You may not feel like paying attention in school. You may not feel like learning. After all, your brain isn't getting the food it needs, either.

What about girls who are overweight? Isn't that bad for your health, too? Don't they need to diet? Even though they are in puberty, wouldn't dieting be better than being too heavy?

Some girls do need to lose weight to be healthy. Being overweight is bad for your health. But during puberty, no girl should be dieting unless her doctor says it's OK.

If you want to go on a diet, see your doctor first. He or she can help you plan a good diet. It will be a diet that lets you lose weight, but still grow up strong and healthy.

Your doctor can also tell if you really *are* overweight. You may not need to diet at all. Fact is, many girls your age think they're too fat when they're not. They are perfectly normal. Why do so many girls think they need to diet when they don't?

Thin, Thin Everywhere
I like the way I look. But a lot of my friends think they're too fat. They want to be as skinny as movie stars and models.

It's not surprising that they do. We all see so

Thousands of skinny-girl images come at us every month.

They send a message. They tell us that we have to be super thin to be beautiful.

After a while, we start to believe it.

many images of thin actresses on TV and in the movies. Super skinny models are everywhere. We see them on billboards and in magazines. We see them over and over and over again. Thousands of skinny-girl images come at us every month. They send a message. They tell us that we have to be super thin to be beautiful. After a while, we start to believe it.

No wonder there's so much talk about dieting. Turn on the TV. Pick up a paper. Look through a magazine. You can't get away from the topic. And your friends may be just as bad. "Oh, my hips are too fat, I have to go on a diet!" How many times have you heard this sort of thing?

All these skinny images and all this diet talk have an effect. It can make you start to wonder, "Am I too fat? Maybe I should go on a diet!"

There's a lot of pressure on young women to be thin. In some girls, this leads to eating disorders. Some of these girls stop eating or eat very little. Others vomit up what they eat on purpose. Still other girls react to these thin images by overeating. They know they can never be super thin. They figure, "I'm never going to look like that. I might as well eat whatever I want." They don't even try to eat sensibly.

Eating Smart
Give your body the energy it needs to grow. Eat enough to satisfy your hunger. Don't eat too much of any one thing. Eat a variety of foods at meals and snacks. That way, you'll be sure your body gets everything it needs to grow strong and healthy. That's eating smart.

Try not to eat too much junk food. Junk food has a lot of sugar or fat (or both!). It doesn't have the nutrients you need. You can't grow strong and healthy on a diet of chips, cookies, candy, and French fries. So make smart food choices. After school, don't wolf down that bag of chips or cookies. Snack on celery sticks with peanut butter. Or have an apple or a bowl of berries.

Here are some more tips to help you eat smart.

Think about Drinks
Cut down on sodas and sugary fruit drinks. Drink LOTS of water. How much water you need depends on how big you are. But experts say you should drink between four and eight glasses of water every day. Fat-free

Don't eat too much of any one thing.

Junk Food

You can still munch on junk once in a while. No one's perfect. Cookies and chips are okay from time to time. But you need to eat smart most of the time. Say you have a candy bar or cookies at lunch. That's fine. But try to even things out. Choose a fruit or veggie for your after-school snack. Get used to eating lots of good foods. After a while, you may not feel like eating the junk foods as much!

or low-fat milk is a good choice, too. Milk has protein and calcium. You need that calcium for strong bones.

Pig Out on Fruits and Veggies

Snack on fruits and raw veggies. Apples, bananas, strawberries, and melons are great. Try vegetables raw. Grate carrots or beets to top off a sandwich or salad. And don't forget the leafy green veggies, too, like spinach and lettuce. Try to have four servings of veggies and three of fruits each day.

Eat More Grains

Cereal, bread, rice, and pasta are all grains. They give you energy. They also have fiber and vitamins. Eat smart by choosing whole wheat over white bread. Skip the sugary cereals. Choose oatmeal and other sugar-free cereals.

Don't Skip Breakfast

You need energy to stay alert and learn in class. It's a fact: Kids who eat a good breakfast do better in school. They are also less likely to be overweight. So start your day with a good breakfast. Try fruit with yogurt or cereal and low-fat milk. Whole-wheat toast with peanut butter and whole-grain waffles are smart choices, too.

Eating smart is one key
to a healthy body.
Exercise is another.

And Exercise, Too

We all need exercise. It helps you
be your best weight. It burns up the
food you eat so it doesn't get stored as fat. It
makes your heart and lungs stronger. It also
helps to put calcium in your bones. So get off
the couch and start moving around!

As we get older, most of us slow down.
Adults are less active than teens. Teens are
less active than young children. It's normal to
slow down as you grow older. But in this
country most people slow down *too* much.
Most adults and teens just don't get enough
exercise.

The problem is worse with girls. They tend to
slow down more than boys. Guess when girls
really start dragging their feet? You're right:
The slow-down often comes during the
puberty years.

Don't let puberty turn you into a coach potato!
Don't stop riding your bike. Keep climbing

*We all need exercise.
It helps you be
your best weight.
It burns up the food
you eat so it doesn't
get stored as fat.
It makes your heart
and lungs stronger.
It also helps to put
calcium in your
bones.*

trees and running around like a little kid. Stay active. Get the exercise you need. Join a sports team at school. Get into jogging. Make it fun. Start a walking club for girls. Learn to ride a unicycle.

How much exercise should you get? Experts say you should be active every day. That might mean games, sports, walking, or dancing. Anything that keeps you moving. You should have at least 30 to 60 minutes of activity each day.

Three times a week you need to do something that really gets you moving. You need to breathe hard. You need to get the heart pumping fast. Try 30 minutes of fast walking or jogging. Sports like volleyball or tennis are great. You don't have to be super jock girl. But you do have to make the effort.

Get in the habit of being active. Girls who stay active during puberty turn into active adults. And that means a longer, healthier, happier life.

What Is a Serving?

1 serving of fruit equals:

- a medium-size piece of fruit
  or
- 1/2 cup of chopped, cooked, or canned fruit
  or
- 3/4 cup of fruit juice

1 serving of vegetables equals:

- 1 cup of raw, leafy green veggies
  or
- 1/2 cup of other vegetables cooked or chopped raw

Q&A

Q **My best friend is tall and skinny. It doesn't seem to matter how much she eats. Sometimes I hate her and everybody like her. It's like some people are born to be thin. How come?**

A You're right. Some people are born to be thin. Doctors tell us there are three basic body shapes. Some girls are tall and thin. Some girls are full and curvy. Some girls are strong and athletic. We can't change our basic body shape. So if you're full and curvy don't try to lose weight and become a skinny model. Full and curvy bodies are beautiful. Tall and lanky bodies are beautiful. And strong and athletic bodies are beautiful, too.

Q **I put on a lot of weight last year. I'm not fat or anything. But I have funny purplish lines on my hips and thighs. I think they might be stretch marks. Why do I have them if I'm not fat? What can I do about them?**

A Sounds like you do have stretch marks. But being fat isn't the reason. Puberty is. You're growing very fast. That's when stretch marks happen. Your skin can't keep up. It gets stretched thin. The result is purple, red, or pink marks in girls with light skin. In dark-skinned girls, the lines may be more tan in color.

Lots of girls have stretch marks. Most of the time they show up on the breasts, thighs, or hips. But they can happen almost anywhere.

First, the bad news. There's nothing you can do to get rid of stretch marks. There's no cream or lotion that can erase them. Don't waste your money on products that claim to get rid of stretch marks. They don't work.

Now, the good news. Stretch marks usually fade over time. In the end, you will hardly be able to see them.

I think my friend has one of those eating disorders. I forget what it's called. She hardly eats anything. She is so thin it's not even funny. And to her, she's too fat. I'm not kidding. She's always saying how she's so fat. She doesn't want to talk about it with me. What should I do? I'm worried about her.

The eating disorder you are asking about is called anorexia (an-oh-REX-ee-ah). Girls with this disorder are too thin. They don't eat enough to have a healthy body. This is a very serious problem. Girls can die from anorexia. I am not a doctor. I can't tell you if your friend has this problem. But I think you are right to be worried.

This isn't a problem for you to solve. You need adult help. Talk to your mom or dad, a teacher, or a guidance counselor about the problem. They can decide how best to get your friend the help she may need.

It may feel like you are "telling" on your friend. In truth, you could be saving her life.

Q I have a friend who eats a lot of food. I mean a lot. Once she ate almost a whole chocolate cake. But she never gets fat. She's just normal weight. She told me her secret way of dieting. She eats a lot. Then she goes to the bathroom and throws up. She says it's easy once you get used to it. She wants me to do it too. Is this an OK way to keep from gaining weight?

A No, this is NOT OK. Your friend has—or is on her way to having—an eating disorder. This disorder is called bulimia (boo-LEE-mee-ah). Girls who have it overeat and then vomit, or use laxatives, to avoid getting fat.

Bulimia is a serious condition. It can rot your teeth. It can tear the lining of your throat. It can ruin your digestive tract. It can even cause heart failure.

Your friend needs help. You can't talk her out of doing this. What you can do is talk to an adult about her problem. It can be your mom or dad, a teacher, or a counselor. Don't think of this as telling on a friend. Think of it as saving a friend's life. Because that's what it is.

six

B.O. and Zits
A Survival Guide

Growing up is great! You get more respect. You get to do more stuff. But I could do without the pimples and B.O.

B.O. (smelly body odor) and zits (pimples) are NOT FUN! They're not on anyone's list of Great-Things-about-Growing-Up.

But during puberty you do sweat more. You also start to make a new kind of sweat. This new sweat changes your body odor. Your skin also makes more oil. This often leads to pimples.

No girl wants pimples or, worse yet, B.O. Still, they can be a part of growing up. But don't worry! This chapter will fill you in on how to treat pimples and avoid B.O.

Sweat is natural?
Are you *sure*
about that?

Sweat and Body Odor

Sweat is natural and healthy. It helps keep you cool when you get too hot. Sweat, by itself, has no odor. But sweat does play a part in making body odor.

Here's what happens. During puberty, you begin to make a new kind of sweat. This new sweat is made in places like your armpits, groin, and feet. These areas don't get much light or air. They are also *very* damp.

Germs like to grow in wet, dark places. And they *love* the new kind of sweat you're making. Yum, yum.

They eat it right up! Then their little germ bodies break the sweat down. Sadly for us, it breaks down into something really stinky. The result is B.O.

B.O. doesn't have to be a big deal. But you do need to shower or take a bath every day. B.O. germs can also live in dirty clothing. So wearing clean clothes is a must.

Showering and wearing clean clothes may be enough for you. If not, try a deodorant. It can cut down the number of B.O. germs. It also covers up bad smells. Most have an anti-perspirant. This keeps you from sweating as much. Be sure to follow directions. If the deodorant causes redness or burning, stop using it.

Oily Hair and Pimples

OK, it's puberty. I'm getting pubic hair. I'm getting boobs. I expected all this. But why is my hair so greasy?

There are glands in your skin that make oil. At puberty, they start to work overtime. They make more oil than ever before. Oil glands in your scalp start working harder, too. They make your hair oilier. You need to shampoo more than you did before.

Here's a Tip

Wear 100% cotton clothes. Cotton "breathes." In other words, it lets air in. Your body stays drier under cotton clothes. There's less chance for B.O. germs to do their stinky work.

It's like Zit City. My face is always breaking out. I don't eat pizza, French fries, chocolate, or any of that stuff. I still get zits. I wash my face a lot. I keep washing my face and they won't go away. Why is puberty doing this to me?

Don't pop (squeeze) your pimples. You may spread germs and make your skin worse.

Pizza, fried foods, and chocolate don't cause pimples. Pimples happen when oil gets trapped under the skin. You have lots of oil glands. They're in almost every part of your skin. You also have little holes in the skin, called pores. They allow oil from the glands to get out onto the skin. These pores can get blocked. Then oil gets trapped under the skin. The result may be pimples, whiteheads, blackheads, or bad acne.

Blackheads look like tiny bits of dirt under the skin. They're not. They are trapped oil that has turned black. Worse yet, germs may grow in the trapped oil. This causes an infection that results in red, swollen pimples. The infection under the skin may spread, causing really bad acne. There may be large, red, and painful bumps on your skin. Now for the good news. There *are* things you can do about these skin problems.

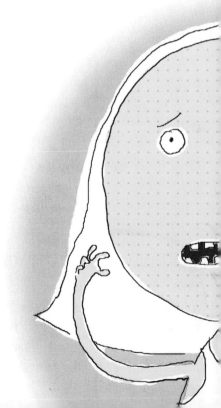

Dealing with Pimples and Acne

Don't pop (squeeze) your pimples. You may spread germs and make your skin worse. Also, popping may leave scars that don't go away.

Now for the good news. There are things you can do about these skin problems.

Your skin is making more oil. It's important to keep your skin clean. But twice a day is enough. Wash your face in the morning and again at bedtime. Don't scrub. Be gentle. Use a mild soap. Pat (don't rub) your face dry.

If you play sports or get real sweaty during the day, you could wash again. But don't overdo it. Washing more isn't going to clear up your acne. Washing can't get at oil trapped *under* your skin. And it's this trapped oil that causes pimples. In fact, too much washing can make things worse. Your skin may get too dry. Then the glands in your skin start making more oil. The result may be even more pimples.

My mom got me this face washing stuff. It didn't help at all. Then she got me this other stuff and it works really well.

At the drugstore, you can buy lots of products for pimples. Read the labels. Look for the words "benzoyl peroxide." It's the best acne treatment you can buy without a doctor's prescription. It fights germs and unblocks pores. It takes some time before you see results. In most cases, it takes about two weeks. But it may take as long as two months. If you don't see results by the end of two months, see your doctor.

Follow the directions. Don't just treat the pimples you have now. Also treat the places where you've had problems in the past. Don't stop treatment when your skin clears up. If you do, the pimples may come back.

Benzoyl peroxide can cause itching and redness. It may even make your skin worse at first. It comes in three strengths—2.5%, 5% and 10% (2.5% is the mildest; 10% is the strongest). Start with the mildest. It will be less likely to bother your skin. After a while, your body may adjust to the medicine. Then, if you need to, switch to the 5% strength. Later, you may need the 10% strength.

Benzoyl peroxide (BEN-zoyl puh-ROK-side):
A lotion you can buy in a drugstore that helps clear up acne

Q **I have pimples. They really bug me. But how do I know if they're bad enough that I need to go to a doctor?**

A Ask yourself these questions. Have you used a drugstore treatment for two months or more, but it hasn't worked? Do your pimples keep you from enjoying your life? Do bad cases of acne run in your family? Did your acne start when you were only nine or ten? Do you have large, red, painful bumps that don't go away? Does your acne leave scars?

Did you answer "yes" to any of these questions? If so, you should see a doctor about your acne.

Q **I want to do something about my pimples. But my parents just say, "It's not that bad. You'll grow out of it." What can I do?**

A True, most of us do grow out of it. But what about the time between now and then? Besides, you don't want to risk ending up with scars.

Take your time when you talk to your parents. Try to explain to them how much it means to you. You might try writing a letter. It's often easier to make your case in writing. You might also want to show them the answer to the question above.

Q I have zits, and not just on my face. They creep down my neck. They're all over my back, chest, and shoulders. Is it normal to have pimples in these places?

A Pimples can occur any place where there are oil glands. And there are plenty of oil glands on the neck, back, chest, and shoulders. These pimples are no different than the pimples on your face. You can treat them in the same way. A product with benzoyl peroxide is best. If this doesn't help, then you should see a doctor.

Q My friend has really gross B.O. People are always going, "What's that smell?" And it's her. I really like her. But kids at school make fun of her when she's not around. Should I tell her?

A If you don't, someone else will. They may not do it as kindly as you will. How you go about telling her is important. It will have a lot to do with how she takes it. It's best done in private, not in front of a group. Here's how two other girls did it.

"We were alone in my bedroom. I said, 'Woooeee, girlfriend, you stink. Use some of this pleeze. Before I die.' I was shoving this big old thing of deodorant at her. I was acting all loud and crazy and laughing. But she got the hint."

"I told my mom and she helped me. My friend was sleeping over. My mom came in and sat on the bed. She gave us this big talk about growing up and body odor and all. She gave us each a little kit, with soap, mouthwash, deodorant, and stuff. My friend thought it was really cool."

seven

What's Up Down There?

A Look at Your Private Parts

Baby girls and baby boys look very much alike. You can't tell which is which—when they have diapers on, that is! But without diapers, it's easy to tell boys from girls. Baby boys have male sex organs. Baby girls have female sex organs.

Another name for a girl's sex organs is the *vulva*. Some people say vagina when they should say vulva. The vagina is a sex organ, too, but it is *inside* the body. Vulva is the correct name for the sex organs on the *outside* of your body.

It's kind of hard for a girl to see her own vulva. So you may not know what yours looks like. But it's easy to find out. Just take a look for yourself.

The Vulva

The picture on the next page shows the parts of a vulva. Of course, we're not all the same. And this shows a grown woman's vulva. So yours isn't going to look just like the one shown here. But we'll tell you how each part of the vulva changes during puberty. This will help you compare your vulva to the one in the picture.

We'll begin at the top of the vulva, with the mons.

The mons is a pad of fat over the pubic bone. In grown women, pubic hair covers the mons. During puberty, the fat pad grows thicker. This makes the mons stick out more. It also gives it a more rounded shape.

Vagina (vah-JEYE-nuh): One of the female sex organs inside the body

Vulva (VUL-vuh): The female sex organs on the outside of the body

The lower part of the mons divides into two folds of skin. They are called the outer lips.

The outer lips are thin and flat in little girls. At puberty, they begin to change. They become thicker and more rounded. Pubic hair also begins to grow here. In fact, the very first hairs grow along the edges of the outer lips.

Of course, we're not all the same. And this shows a grown woman's vulva. So yours isn't going to look just like the one shown here.

Look at the undersides of these lips. There is no pubic hair. The skin is smooth. It is not as dry as the skin on the mons. You may see small, light dots just below the skin. These are oil glands.

In between the outer lips, you'll find the inner lips. Both the inner and outer lips are sometimes called vaginal lips.

The inner lips change at puberty, too. They grow bigger. They change color. They get more wrinkly. You can't see them, but there are oil glands here, too.

The outer lips cover the inner lips. But in some of us, the inner lips stick out beyond the outer lips. One of the inner

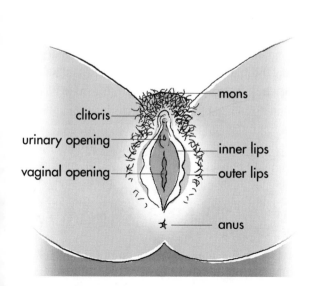

clitoris

urinary opening

vaginal opening

mons

inner lips

outer lips

anus

Taking a Look

You'll need a mirror. A hand mirror works well. You'll also need good light.

You may feel funny about looking at this part of your body. After all, they are called private parts. But private means private to other people. It doesn't mean that you can't look at your own vulva.

When you're ready, find a place where you can be alone. It might be your bedroom. It might be the bathroom. Get comfortable. Make sure you have enough light. Hold the mirror between your legs. Take a good look.

lips may be bigger than the other. It's all perfectly normal!

The inner lips join at the top. They form a hood, or cover. Under this hood, you may see or feel a little bump. This is the tip of the clitoris.

The clitoris, too, grows larger during puberty. You can't see all of the clitoris. Most of it lies inside your body, under your skin. The tip is the only part you can see. And, to see it, you may have to pull back the hood.

At times, the tip of the clitoris "peeks" out from under the hood. At other times, it is totally hidden under the hood. But it's easy to pull back the hood and see the tip.

In grown women, the tip is about the size of the eraser on a pencil. Of course, you aren't fully grown yet. Yours may be smaller.

The clitoris has many nerve endings. It is *very* sensitive. In fact, the inner lips, the outer lips, and the whole vulva are all sensitive. Touching this area of the body can give us tingly, "sexy" feelings.

The inner lips protect two openings that lie

It's kind of hard for a girl to see her own vulva.
So you may not know what yours looks like.
But it's easy to find out. Just take a look for yourself.

between them. Move straight down from the clitoris. You will come to the first opening. It is called the urinary opening.

The urinary opening is not a sex organ. But it is part of the vulva. It's the place where urine or "pee," leaves the body.

The opening looks like an upside down V. It gets bigger during puberty. But it's still not very large. It can be hard to find. Be sure to move straight down from the clitoris. It's the first dimpled area you come to. Keep looking, it's there for sure.

Keep moving down. You will come to the second opening. It is the opening to the vagina. The vagina itself is up inside the body. But its opening is part of the vulva.

The vaginal opening also

gets larger during puberty. You may expect to see inside of the vagina. After all, it's an opening. You should be able to look through an opening and see what's in there. But it doesn't work like that.

The vagina is not a hollow space inside the body. It's like a sleeve. When your arm is not inside, the sleeve is flat. The front and back of the inner sleeve lie flat against each other. So do the inside walls of the vagina.

Now pretend you put a rubber band around the sleeve about an inch from the cuff. Then try to look inside the sleeve.

Now pretend you put a rubber band around the sleeve about an inch from the cuff. Then try to look inside the sleeve. You'd see folds of material all bunched up by the rubber band.

The rubber band is like the muscles that circle the vaginal opening. If you look into the vaginal opening, you don't see a black hole. You see folds of flesh from the inner walls of the vagina. They are all bunched together by the muscles that circle the opening.

In fact, you may not even see too much of this. Your hymen may be in the way.

The hymen is a thin piece of tissue. It lies just inside the vaginal opening. Hymens are not all alike. Some are just a ruffle around the lower part of the vaginal opening. Some stretch across the opening, but have one or more openings.

Before puberty, the hymen is thin and very hard to see. It grows thicker and gets wrinkly during puberty. It may still be difficult for you to find it.

There's another opening in this part of your body. It's the anus. This is the place where feces, or "poop," leaves the body. It's not part of the vulva. It's further back. But it is nearby, so we thought we'd point it out.

That ends your tour of your vulva. Now let's talk about yet another way the vulva changes during puberty.

More Moist

Once puberty starts, you may notice that your vulva seems more moist. You may have a new feeling of wetness in this area.

No, we don't mean wet, like wetting your pants wet. We mean the vulva is damper. It is a little moister than it was before. Here's why.

Remember the oil glands in the vaginal lips?

Say What?

Some people say vagina when they should say vulva.

The vagina is a sex organ, too, but it is *inside* the body.

Vulva is the correct name for the sex organs on the *outside* of your body.

"Are You Sure I Have a Hymen?"

In young girls the hymen may be very hard to see. During puberty it gets thicker. But you still may have trouble finding it. Sometimes the hymen is nothing more than a little fringe of tissue just inside the vaginal opening. Also, there are lots of folds and bulges of flesh in the area. It can be hard to tell what's what.

But even if you can't find it, it's there. Rarely, if ever, is a girl born without a hymen. In any case, it's nothing to worry about. A hymen doesn't "do" anything. You don't need one. If you want to be sure it's there, ask your doctor to point it out to you.

Before puberty, these glands don't make oil. Then, puberty hits. These glands start to work. The oil they make changes the odor of your body. It also makes the skin in the area moist. It's part of the reason the vulva has this new feeling of wetness.

Also, you may begin to have some vaginal discharge. This is a small amount of white or clear fluid. It comes from the vaginal opening. When it dries, it may leave a yellow stain on your panties. It starts about a year or two before your first period. And it's perfectly normal! We'll explain more about it in Chapter 8. We wanted to say something about it here because it, too, adds to the feeling of wetness in the vulva.

During puberty, this area of your body becomes very sensitive. It responds to "sexy" thoughts and feelings, and to touch. One way it responds is by making some clear, slippery fluid. These fluids are a perfectly normal response of your body. They also add to the new feeling of wetness in the vulva.

My friend told me she has a funny smell down there. I said it happens to me, too. So now we want to know, "What's the best way to keep that area clean?"

If you keep the vulva clean, there shouldn't be any odor problem. Wash this area every day when you wash the rest of your body. Use a mild soap and lots of warm water. Here's another thing you need to know to keep this area clean. Feces (poop) can have germs. The anus is not far from the urinary and the vaginal openings. You don't want germs to get into these openings. So when you go to the bathroom, wipe from front to back. Start with the vulva and move back toward the anus. Do the same when you wash in this area.

If you wash every day and still have a bad odor, you may have a vaginal infection. Besides odor, there may be other signs. Itching or burning in the area are also signs. A discharge that is any color other than clear or white is another. If you have one or more of these signs, see a doctor. In most cases, these infections are easy to treat.

Don't use vaginal deodorants. (These are also called feminine hygiene sprays.) They can cause rashes. They can lead to infections. They can also cover up odor that is a sign of an infection.

You shouldn't douche either. (To douche means to wash out the vagina.) Your vagina has natural ways of keeping itself clean. By douching you may upset the vagina's natural way of preventing infections.

Sometimes I touch myself down there and it feels good. Is this bad for me?

No. This is a very sensitive area. Touching yourself here feels good. Touching or rubbing yourself in this way is called masturbation (MASS-tur-BAY-shun). There's nothing harmful in doing it.

Most of us masturbate at one time or another. Some girls start when they're young and continue for all their lives. Others start when they are older. Some girls masturbate quite often. Other girls never, or hardly ever, masturbate. It's OK if you do and it's OK if you don't.

If you masturbate, you may have an orgasm. It's hard to describe just what an orgasm feels like. Some people say it's like a shivery feeling that goes through the body. It's a very good feeling. You may not have an orgasm (OR-gaz-uhm) when you masturbate. It may take a bit of practice.

Some people don't masturbate because of their religious or moral beliefs. And that's OK, too.

eight

The Inside Story
Changes You Can't See

You change in many ways as you grow up. You get taller. You get heavier. You grow breasts and pubic hair. You know when these changes are happening. You can see them with your own eyes.

During puberty, there are also changes you *can't* see. They happen *inside* your body. You won't be able to see them for yourself. Even so, you will know they are happening. There will be outer signs of these inner changes.

Getting your first period is one of these signs. In this chapter, we'll tell you why and how periods happen. We'll also tell you more about the changes you can't see. By the time we're done, you'll know a lot more about puberty, inside and out.

What's going on in there?

On the Inside

In the last chapter, we talked about the female parts on the outside of your body. They are called the vulva. Here, we'll be talking about the female parts on the inside of your body. They are called reproductive organs.

An organ is a part of your body that does a certain job. The heart is an organ. It pumps blood. The lungs are organs. They let you breathe.

The reproductive organs have a job, too. They let you reproduce. To reproduce means to have a baby. In other words, these organs let a woman have a baby.

Even a child has reproductive organs. But a child's organs aren't fully grown. They're not mature. That's why a child can't have a baby. During puberty, these organs mature. Once they do, your body is able to have a baby.

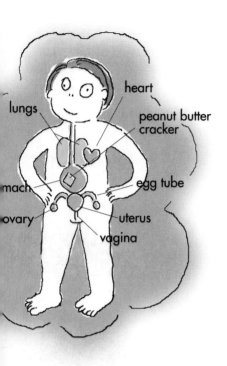

lungs
heart
peanut butter cracker
mach
egg tube
ovary
uterus
vagina

Does that mean you are ready to be a parent? No, not by a long shot! But one day you may be ready. There may come a time in your life when you decide to have a baby. During puberty, your body is getting ready for that time.

Your Reproductive Organs

Let's talk about each of these organs. See if you can find them in the drawing above.

You have two ovaries, one on each side. They are oval shaped. Each ovary holds hundreds of thousands of ova. Ova are also called eggs. But don't think they are like chicken eggs. They're not…except for one thing. Both the baby chick and the human baby begin life as a mother's egg.

The uterus is a hollow organ. There are two egg tubes attached to the uterus, one on each side. The uterus is not very big. During puberty it grows bigger. In a grown woman it's the size of a pear. It's shaped like a pear, too—an upside-down pear.

The lower part of the uterus is like the neck of the pear. This part is called the cervix. A tiny tunnel runs through the cervix. It leads from inside the uterus to the top of the vagina.

The vagina connects the uterus and cervix to the outside of the body. The cervix fits into the upper end of the vagina. The lower end of the vagina opens on the outside of the body. Maybe you remember the name of that opening. It's the vaginal opening. We talked about it in Chapter 7. It's part of the vulva.

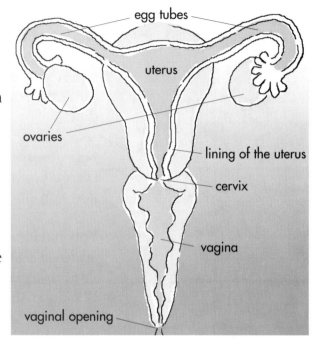

The Stork Didn't Bring You

The uterus, cervix, and vagina are all connected. They have to be. That's how we come into this world.

The uterus is where a baby grows before it is born. It holds the baby and keeps it warm and safe. As the baby gets larger, so does the uterus. It stretches and stretches. After nine months or so, the baby is big enough to be born.

The tunnel inside the cervix is very tiny. But it, too, can stretch to many times its normal size. When the baby is going to be born, the tunnel gets wider. It stretches wide enough for the baby to pass through.

Now the baby is about to be born. Mom pushes with all her might. The uterus squeezes hard. The baby is pushed through the cervix and into the vagina. Luckily, that's very stretchy, too. The baby is pushed through it. Then here comes baby out the vaginal opening into the world. Hello, baby!

As you can see, these organs have to stretch a lot when a baby is born. Before puberty, they're not very stretchy. But during puberty, the cervix and vagina become more stretchy. They also become moist. Because they are moist, they stay nice and stretchy. (Things that dry out tend to get stiff and not stretch very well.)

Vaginal Discharge

I haven't started my period yet. But sometimes I notice this creamy white stuff down there.

This girl is having vaginal discharge. About a year or two before your first period, your body begins making a small amount of fluid. This is the fluid that keeps your vagina and cervix moist. It also keeps your vagina clean. Vaginal discharge leaves the body through the vaginal opening. That's why it's called vaginal discharge.

> **Vaginal discharge (VAJ-in-uhl dis-CHARJ):**
> A clear or white fluid that comes from the vagina

Vaginal discharge is either clear or white. When it dries on panties, it may be a pale yellow color. Some girls don't have much discharge. They don't even notice it. But many girls do.

Surprise, surprise. The stork didn't bring you.

You may have more discharge on some days than others. In any case, it's a sign that you're changing inside.

Inside the Uterus

The inside of the uterus has a special lining. In the early weeks of pregnancy, this lining is very important. It "feeds" the growing baby.

Don't look at me! I didn't bring the baby.

Before puberty, the lining of the uterus is thin. During puberty, it starts to grow. It grows thick and rich in the nutrients a developing baby needs. This lining will help cushion and feed a developing baby.

The lining grows so the uterus will be ready if you get pregnant. But you and I know that won't happen for *ages*! It will be *years* before you're ready to even think about being a mom. Does this fancy lining just sit there waiting until you are ready to start a family? No, it doesn't.

Since the lining is not needed, the uterus gets rid of it. It sheds the lining. Then it starts growing a new one. It takes about a month for the uterus to shed the old lining and grow a new one.

Of course, you're not going to be pregnant the next month, either. That means you won't need the new lining. So the uterus sheds that one, too. Then it grows another new one. Then it sheds that lining and grows another one.

*But you and I know it will be **years** before you're ready to even think about being a mom.*

If you do get pregnant, the lining of the uterus isn't shed. The cycle of shedding and growing stops. A few months after the baby is born, it starts up again. It goes on and on. The cycle finally stops when you are too old to have a baby. For most women, this happens between the ages of 45 and 55.

Shedding the Lining
The lining isn't shed all at once. It takes a number of days. Here's how it happens.

First, the blood supply to the lining cuts off. Within a couple of days, the lining begins to fall apart. Pieces of it break off and slide down to the uterus. Soon the lining is only a bloody pool at the bottom of the uterus.

The tiny tunnel in the cervix opens up a bit. It doesn't open much. But it's enough. The bloody fluid drips down into the vagina. Then it slowly comes out through the vaginal opening.

Can you guess what we call this?

Having Your Period

That's right. It's called menstruation, or having your period. Your period is just the lining of your uterus leaving the body.

It takes a number of days for all the bloody fluid to leave your body. Periods usually last for three to five days. But it may take only two days for all the bloody fluid to leave your body. Or, it may take up to nine days.

The bloody fluid is called the menstrual flow or menstrual blood. But it's not just blood. There may also be bits of tissue. You may have some thick, jelly-like blobs in your flow. They're called clots. They may sound gross, but they're perfectly normal.

Your menstrual blood may be red or pink or even brown. It may seem like there's a lot of it. But only about 1/3 of a cup comes out. And that's not just for one day. That's for your whole period.

Menstruation (men-stroo-AY-shun):
The breaking down and shedding of the lining of the uterus

Menstrual flow (MEN-stroo-uhl flo):
The bloody fluid that leaves the body during your period

The amount of blood can vary from day to day during your period. Most of the blood leaves your body in the first few days. Then the bleeding tends to get lighter until your period stops. But not all women follow this pattern. And your pattern may change from one month to the next. We'll talk more about periods in a few pages. First, we want to talk about the ovaries.

The Ovaries

You are born with hundreds of thousands of eggs in your ovaries. But these eggs are not mature. During puberty, the first of these eggs will fully mature. When an egg is fully mature, it pops off the ovary. When a ripe egg pops off the ovary, it is called ovulation.

Ovulation (ahv-you-LAY-shun):
When a mature egg pops off the ovary

Girls ovulate for the first time during puberty. A grown woman ovulates about once a month. But a girl usually doesn't ovulate this often. It may take a few years before a girl starts to ovulate regularly.

Women don't ovulate when they are pregnant. And most women stop ovulating between the ages of 45 to 55. But for most of their adult lives, women ovulate about once a month. Ovulation happens about two weeks before a woman's period. The ovaries "take turns." One month, the right ovary produces the mature egg. The next month, it's the left ovary.

After the mature egg pops off the ovary, it is "caught" by the closest egg tube. The egg then travels through the egg tube to the uterus. It takes about four days for the egg to get there. Once it does, one of two things will happen.

If a woman is going to have a baby, the egg plants itself in the rich, thick lining of the uterus. The lining feeds and cushions the egg as it begins to develop. Over the next nine months, the egg grows into a baby. When you're older and you need more information, you can check out *The "What's Happening to My Body?" Book for Girls*.

Most of the time the woman isn't going to have a baby. The egg floats around inside the uterus for a day or so. Then it just dissolves. Since there's not going to be a baby, the lining of the uterus isn't needed. It begins to break down into the bloody fluid. The fluid seeps through the cervix and vagina. It leaves the body through the vaginal opening. This marks the beginning of the menstrual period.

The period usually lasts for three to five days. Then the menstrual flow stops. By this time, the ovary is already getting another egg ready for ovulation. The uterus is starting to grow a new lining.

About a month after she last ovulated, a woman will ovulate again. The egg travels to the uterus. Once there, it usually dissolves. Then the lining breaks down into the bloody fluid. The fluid comes out the vaginal opening and another period begins.

The Menstrual Cycle
You have a period. You grow a new lining in the uterus. You ovulate. You shed the lining. You have another period. There's a name for this. It's called the menstrual cycle. It repeats itself over and over again.

The menstrual cycle begins with your period. The first day of your period is Day One of your menstrual cycle. The cycle continues until the first day of bleeding of your next period. You can tell how long a cycle is. Just count from the first day of one period to the first day of the next period.

How long is a cycle? Let's say your period starts on May 1. You bleed for four more days. The bleeding stops on May 5. Your next period starts on May 29. Your cycle was 28 days long.

In grown women, a menstrual cycle lasts about a month. The average is 28 days. But anywhere from 21 to 35 days is normal. The length of the cycle may change from one month to the next. Few women have periods that come exactly the same number of days apart every time.

In young girls, menstrual cycles may not be very regular. You may have more than 35 days between periods. It may be months or even a year between periods. Or cycles may be shorter than 21 days. It's normal for a girl's periods to be irregular at first. It may take a few years for your cycle to get at all regular.

It's easy to tell how long a cycle is. Just count from the first day of one period to the first day of the next period.

How long is a cycle? Let's say your period starts on May 1. You bleed for four more days. The bleeding stops on May 5. Your next period starts on May 29. Your cycle was 28 days long.

I got my first period three months ago. But I haven't had one since. What's happening?

When girls first start, their periods usually don't come every month. It may be two or three months between periods, or even a year. Or two periods may come very close together. And the periods may be longer or shorter than usual. There just isn't always a regular cycle at the beginning. All this is normal for a girl who is just starting.

It's different for girls who are already having regular periods. If they go for three months or longer without having a period, they should see a doctor. (If there's any chance she might be pregnant, she should see a doctor right away.)

It was at least a week after my period had ended. Then I saw a little blood spot on my panties. Is this OK?

Some girls do bleed a little between periods. It happens around the time the egg leaves its ovary. It's called "spotting" and it's normal. Still, it's a good idea to tell your doctor.

Bleeding quite a bit between periods can be a sign of a medical problem. If this happens, you should see a doctor. "Quite a bit" means more than a little spot for one or two days. Chances are, it's not serious. But get it checked out.

Q **Is it true that women who live together have their periods at the same time of the month?**

A This is a very old belief. And it may be true. One study looked at women who live together. It turned out that women who spend lots of time together sometimes have their periods at the same time. But this was only one study. So you may get your period at the same time as family members or close friends. Or you may not.

nine

That Time of the Month
All about Getting Your Period

I was thirteen when it happened. It was during English class. I had a feeling of wetness. I went to the bathroom. "Oh, it's my period!" I was kind of scared, but not too scared. My mom had talked to me about it, so I knew what was going on. Besides, some of my friends already had their periods. I folded up some toilet paper and used it like a pad. I went back to class and acted like nothing had happened. Nobody said anything. After class I told my best friend about it. She was happy for me.

Having your first period can be very exciting! But it can also be a little scary and confusing. This chapter will tell you what to expect. It will tell you all about pads, tampons, cramps, and something called PMS. By the end, you'll know much more about having a period.

First Period, When?

Most girls get their first period between the ages of 11 and 14. Twelve or 13 is the average. But some girls are only nine or even younger. Others don't get their periods until they are 16 or even older.

I had my first period when I was 13. And my daughter had her first period when she was

I got my first period when I was 12.

I got my first period when I was 11.

Hey, I did, too!

I was 15 before I ever got mine.

Still waiting. But I' really not in too b a hurry.

13. Daughters often start at about the same age as their moms. But they don't always.

You can get a clue about when you'll have your first period from your mom. You can get clues from your own body as well. Here are some things to look for.

Have your breasts started to develop? Your period will probably start three to three and a half years after you get breast buds. (Remember those? See the stages of breast development on pages 22-23.) In fact, most girls are in Breast Stage 4 when they get their periods. But some girls are only in Stage 3. Others don't get theirs until Stage 5.

I was ten!

I was 13!

Mine just started last month. I'm 11.

Uh...mine started when I was 12.

Not really! I haven't ever had one.

Do you have any pubic hairs? The first pubic hairs are soft and thin. Your period will probably come two and a half to four and a half years after your first pubic hairs.

Have you noticed any vaginal discharge (see page 85)? This is a sign that your period is not too far away. Most girls get their first period six to 12 months after the start of this discharge. But it may be two years or even longer.

First Period, Where?
Sure, it's OK if you start at home and nobody sees you. But what if it happens to me at school?

I thought there was going to be a lot of blood, like a dam had broken. But it was only a few drops. When I went to the bathroom there was this stain on my panties. And that was it.

Girls often worry about *where* they will get that first period. They wonder if it will be embarrassing to them. But for most girls, the

You may worry that your first period will happen at school. You can always just use a wad of toilet paper inside your panties. No one needs to know.

first period is very light. There might be a few spots of bright red blood or a brown sticky stain on their panties. It's just not that much at first.

With their first period, most girls don't feel the flow coming out. At most, there's a feeling of dampness in their panties. Many don't even feel that. They just see a little blood on the toilet paper or on their panties when they go to the bathroom. That's when they find out they have gotten their periods.

Also, you can be prepared. You can carry a pad with you. Keep it in your locker at school. Or carry it in your purse or backpack.

If you don't have a pad with you, don't panic. At school you can ask a teacher, the nurse, or a lady in the office for one. Public bathrooms often have machines that sell pads. You can always just use a wad of toilet paper inside your panties.

With a little care, no one needs to know when you have your first period. At least not until you tell them.

Telling Mom or Dad

My mom and I have always been able to talk about puberty and those things. So I told her right away when I got my period. She was real happy.

I never talked to my mom about sex and private things. I think she's bashful. When I finally started my period, I didn't know how to tell her.

My mom and dad are separated. I live with my dad. Once he tried to have "the talk" with me. But it got kind of embarrassing for both of us. I got my period three weeks ago, and I still haven't been able to tell him.

Some girls find it easy to tell their parents about getting their first period. For others it may be hard. It sort of depends on how much you and your parents talk together.

It's a good idea to talk to your mom or dad when you get your period. Your mom can answer your questions. She can be a good friend during this time in your life.

Many girls find it hard to talk to their dads. Of course, he won't be able to tell you about his first period. But he might surprise you by how

Some ideas to help you talk with either your mom or dad:

Try the direct approach. Just say, "Hey, guess what happened to me. I got my period." Remember that you might not be the only one who's embarrassed. Also, embarrassment doesn't last forever. Once you break the ice and start talking, it gets easier.

Ask about what happened to them. "Mom, how did you tell grandma when you got your first period?"

"Dad, was it easy for you to talk to your parents about puberty?"

"Do you wish it had been easier to talk to them?"

Try talking in the car.

Lots of kids and parents say it's easier to talk about things in the car. Why? Maybe because you don't have to look at each other.

Write a note.

Sometimes it's easier to say things in a note. Keep the note simple. Tell them you've had your first period. Make a short list of questions. Tell them you want to talk to them.

Pick a good time.

Make it private. Try to find time when they're not busy with other things. Chances are they'll be real happy for you. They may even want to celebrate the happy event.

much he knows. Besides, this can be a special time. It can be a time when you and he start talking more about "important" things.

Celebrate!

When the girls in my family get their period, my grandma sends them a pearl necklace. It's a symbol.

My mom told my dad about my first period. It surprised me how excited he was. He took me out for dinner. It was just him and me.

I was really excited when I got it. I spent the whole afternoon writing in my diary. I wrote about all it means to me and what I want for my life.

Having your first period is special. It's an important step in growing up. It shows that you're becoming a woman.

When you tell your parents, they may want to do something special. It could be anything. Your dad might cook your favorite meal. Your mom might take you out to dinner. She might give you a present. It might be something you could pass on to your daughter someday. You might go on a trip or take a walk in the moonlight. It doesn't matter so much what

Celebrate Yourself!

If your parents aren't the celebrating type, that's OK. Celebrate with your girl friends. It matters that you let people know. It matters that you feel special inside yourself. Write about how you feel in your diary. Buy yourself a present. And, congratulations from me!

you do. It matters that you celebrate your first period.

Pads

Pad and tampons soak up the blood from your periods. They protect your panties from stains. Most girls start with pads, so we will, too.

Pads are easy to use. They are held in place by sticky strips. You peel the paper off the sticky strip. Then press the pad, sticky side down, onto your panties.

Don't put the pad too far forward or too far back. If you do, you could have stains in the front or back of your panties. If you have a problem no matter where you put the pad, try one of the longer pads. If you have stains on the sides, try a pad with "wings" on the sides. Or try a pad made for a heavier flow.
On the outside of the package, you'll find an "absorbency rating." This gives you an idea of how much flow the pad can absorb, or soak up. Different companies use different ratings. But the most absorbent pads are the ones that say "overnight." The next rating is usually called "heavy." Then there's usually a "regular" or "medium" rating.

Some companies have a line of thin or ultra-thin pads. The same ratings apply to these pads. For example, the ones rated heavy can absorb a lot, even though they are very thin.

Most pads are rectangles. But some have rounded ends. Some pads are curved or "contoured." This is supposed to make them fit better. Some pads are made for girls. They have words like "slender" or "junior" on the package.

There are so many different brands on the market. It's hard to know which to buy! Talk to your mom, other women, and girls you know. Find out what they use and why. Then try different ones to find out what you like.

You don't have to get up at night to change your pad. During the day, change it every four to six hours. Change it more often on days of heavy flow. Fresh blood from your period doesn't have a bad odor. But when it comes in contact with air, germs can start to grow. And it's these germs that cause odor. So change your pad even if it isn't soaked with blood. Then there won't be any bad smells.

Don't flush pads or their wrappers down the toilet! They can clog the toilet. Wrap the

Pads are easy to use. They are held in place by sticky strips. You peel the paper off the sticky strip. Then press the pad, sticky side down, onto your panties.

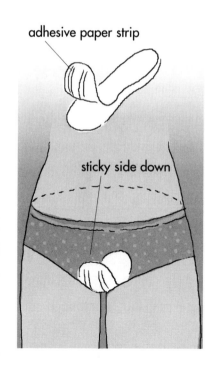

adhesive paper strip

sticky side down

pad with a tissue or toilet paper. Then toss it in the trash.

Tampons

A tampon is a tight roll of cotton or other material. You put it inside your vagina. It soaks up the flow before it leaves your body. Some girls start using tampons with their first period. A tampon gives you more freedom than a pad. You can even go swimming.

A tampon gives you more freedom than a pad. You can even go swimming.

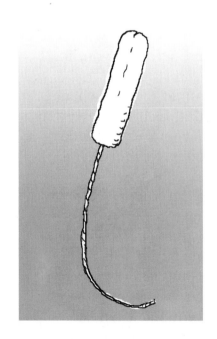

Just like pads, some tampons absorb more blood than others. Look for the "absorbency rating" on the box. Tampons rated "junior" or "light" are made for light flow days. They absorb the least blood. "Regular" tampons are for light or medium flow days. "Super" tampons are good for medium to heavy flow. Those rated "super plus" are for very heavy flow. "Ultra" tampons are for super heavy flow. They absorb the most blood.

When you first use tampons, choose one with a junior, or light, rating. They are the thinnest. That means they are the easiest to put into the vagina.

As your period gets more regular, choose the tampon with the right absorbency for your flow. Don't use a tampon that's more absorbent than you need. If you have a light flow, don't use a super tampon. If you do, you may have trouble removing it. It won't have enough blood in it to slide out of your vagina easily. It may stick and pull at the vagina.

Remember that your flow may be heavier on some days than on others. You may need tampons with different ratings for different days.

Tampons should be changed every four to eight hours. It's safer to use a pad overnight. That way you don't have to worry about sleeping past the eight-hour limit.

You can't feel the tampon once it's in place. It's easy to forget to remove a tampon. If you do forget, don't panic. Just take it out as soon as you remember.

So, there are three rules to follow with tampons. First, try your best not to leave one in more than eight hours. Second, don't use a tampon that's more absorbent than you need. And, third, switch to pads for overnight. Following these rules lowers your risk of getting something called TSS.

TSS is short for Toxic Shock Syndrome. It is a rare, but serious, infection. It can happen to

Toxic Shock Syndrome (TOX-sik shok SIN-drome): A very rare but sometimes deadly infection that's connected to using tampons

women and girls who are using tampons. TSS sounds scary. But don't forget, it is a *very* rare disease. Still, it's good to do everything you can to lower your risk. Be sure to read the info on TSS that comes in each package.

Putting in Tampons

Are you thinking of using tampons? If so, you need to know about applicators. Some tampons come inside an applicator. The applicator helps you get the tampon into your vagina.

Each brand is a little different. But most applicators are made of two tubes. The tampon is packed in the larger, outer tube. The second, inner tube is smaller. It pushes the tampon out of the larger tube and into the vagina. Once the tampon is in place, you throw away the two tubes. You can flush a used tampon. But don't put the applicator in the toilet.

Some tampons don't have applicators. You just push them into place with your finger.

Learning to put a tampon in is like learning anything. It may take a few tries to get the hang of it. Once the tampon is in place, you won't feel it. Read the directions that come with the tampon. Here are some tips that may help.

Each brand is a little different. Most applicators are made of two tubes. Some tampons don't have applicators. You just push them into place with your finger.

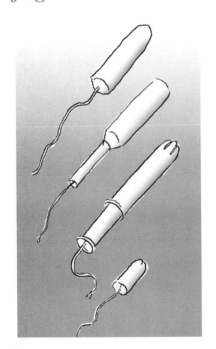

Waste one. Unwrap a tampon and fool with it. Take it apart. Look at it. See how it works. Put it in a glass of water. Watch it grow. Then throw it away.

Know where it's going. Go back to page 75. It tells how to use a mirror to find the opening to your vagina. Put a finger inside the opening. Tighten your muscles around your finger. These muscles keep the tampon from falling out. But you have to push the tampon in far enough to get past these muscles. If you don't, the muscles will just clamp down on the tampon. This won't hurt anything. But it won't feel very comfortable.

Head in the right direction. Your vagina isn't straight up and down. It's at an angle. Point the tampon toward the small of your back. (That's the lower, curving part of your back just above your fanny.)

Relax! If you're tense, you make the muscles of the vagina tighter. This makes it hard (or

Unwrap a tampon and fool with it. Take it apart. Look at it. See how it works. Put it in a glass of water. Watch it grow. Then throw it away.

impossible!) to put in the tampon. So, relax. Take a few slow, deep breaths. Relax those muscles as you breathe out.

Make it easier. Use a little saliva (spit) or KY jelly on the tip of the tampon. This will help it slide in more easily.

Now do it! Spread apart the inner lips with one hand. With the other hand, gently push the tip of the outer tube into the opening of the vagina. (If you have any pain, stop. Don't force it.) Then, with your index finger, push the smaller tube up into the larger tube. This pushes the tampon out of the applicator and into your vagina.

If one hand doesn't work, try two. If the above is too hard for you, try using both hands to push the tubes together. One hand holds the larger tube in place. The other hand pushes the smaller tube. But don't hold the larger tube too tightly. You don't want to pinch or narrow the tube. If you

Learning to put a tampon in is like learning anything. It may take a few tries to get the hang of it.

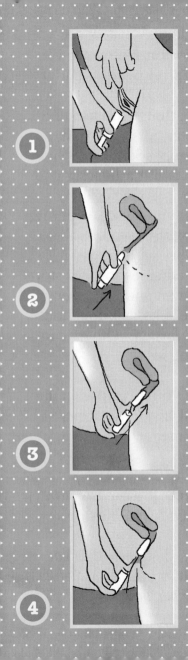

do, the smaller tube can't be pushed in.

Pull the string. A short string should be hanging out of the opening of the vagina. When you're ready to take out the tampon, pull on this string. If you have trouble, you may be taking out the tampon too soon. It may not be wet enough to slide out easily. Try again in another hour or two.

Sometimes the string will work its way up into the vagina. No need to panic! A tampon can't "get lost" inside you. It's still in the vagina. Just reach up into the vagina and pull out the string. Can't find it? Bear down hard (like you were taking a poop). This should bring the tampon and string within reach.

Cramps

Some girls hardly ever have cramps. Others have them with almost every period.

Cramps come just before or during your period. They are felt in the lower belly. The pain may spread around to your back. Or it may go down your legs.

For most girls, cramps are only mild. But some girls have really bad cramps. Some have to stay home from school for a day. If your

Some PMS Symptoms:

Breasts: Heavy, sore, swollen

Skin: Pimples or acne

Aches and pains: Cramps, backache, headache, joint pains

Food: Eating more, food cravings (for chocolate, sweets, or salty foods)

Swelling: Your body holds fluids, causing swelling in breasts, tummy, and ankles, and weight gain

Mental: Tired out, forget things, hard to pay attention

The Blues: Crying, sad, unhappy, feeling bad about yourself

Moody: Cranky, touchy, angry, tense

cramps keep you from doing what you normally do, see your doctor. He or she can treat the problem. There's no need to suffer.

You can do some simple things to ease the pain of cramps. Heat helps relax the tight muscles that go with cramps. Some girls find it's best to curl up in bed with a heating pad. Or you can take a warm, relaxing bath. Exercise can help. Stretching exercises during your period can be especially good.

Drugstores sell lots of medicines to help stop the pain of cramps. But you should *never take them on your own*. Some, like aspirin, should never be used by girls your age. Others can only be used in certain doses.

Tell your mom or dad if you have bad cramps. They know your medical history. Let them give you the right medicine.

PMS

I know my period's coming. My breasts start hurting. I get zits. I get really touchy, too.

Yeah, I get these cravings. I just want to eat sweets, and it's like, what's going on? It's like a sign. I'm going to get my period.

Many of us have signs, or symptoms, in the week or so before our periods. For most of us, they aren't a problem. They just tell us our periods are coming. But for some of us these symptoms are a problem.

PMS is short for premenstrual syndrome. It is a catchall name for a long list of symptoms. Some are listed here. A woman with PMS may have one or more of these symptoms each month. They start three to ten days before her period. Most of the time, they go away once the period starts.

PMS mostly happens in women over 20. It is very rare in girls your age. But you may have some of the symptoms on this list. If so, don't take any of the PMS treatments sold in drug-stores on your own. They may have drugs harmful to girls your age. Ask your parents before taking anything for PMS.

Diet and exercise can really help with PMS. Re-read the part on eating and exercise in Chapter 5 (pages 51-62). Avoid salt and sugar. Don't use caffeine. (It's not just in coffee. It's in many teas and soft drinks, too.) And be sure to get plenty of sleep.

Premenstrual Syndrome (pre-MEN-stroo-uhl SIN-drome): A group of signs, or symptoms, that women may have before or during their periods

Q&A

Q I wear pads when I get my period. But it feels like there's a towel between my legs. Will other people see that I'm wearing a pad?

A Have you tried the thin or ultra-thin pads? They won't feel like a towel. You may think people can tell when you're wearing a pad. But they can't. Stand in front of a mirror. We bet you can't see a bulge from the pad. No one else can either.

Q If the hymen covers your vaginal opening, how can you get a tampon in?

A The hymen has one or more openings in it. This is where blood from your period leaves your body. There is usually an opening big enough for a tampon.

Q I haven't started yet. But is it OK to use a tampon when I have my first period?

A Yes. In fact, many girls use tampons for their first period. Just make sure it's a junior size, designed to fit a young girl's vagina.

Q I'm eight and a half years old and in the third grade. I just had my first period. None of my friends have started. Am I OK?

Eight and a half is young to start having periods. If a girl is less than nine when her period starts, we tell her to see a doctor. So tell your mom you should see a doctor. Chances are there's nothing wrong, but get it checked out.

I'm 14, but I haven't started yet. At school it seems that all my friends do is talk about their periods. The other day I couldn't help it. I told them that I had my period. Now I feel really guilty, like I did something really bad. Was it wrong to lie to them?

Sure, you let a little fib slip out. But I don't think it's all that bad. Your lie didn't hurt anyone else. And you won't have to live with it forever. Some day soon you will get your period. Then it won't matter if you were the last kid in your class. Remember that some girls don't get their periods until they are 16 or even older. But if you are very worried about it, tell one of your parents or an older sister. And mention it the next time you see your doctor for a check- up.

I have really heavy periods. It's not just the first day or so. It's my whole period. I got my period when I was ten. So it's almost two years. Right from the start I bled a whole lot. How much bleeding is too much?

Bleeding through a pad or tampon every hour is too much bleeding. I mean really soaking through. (And not just a panty liner or junior tampon.) Use the most absorbent tampon or pad. If you soak through one of these every hour, call your doctor.

Your periods shouldn't last more than ten days. If it does, that's too much bleeding. You should see a doctor.

Some of us just have heavy periods. It's normal for our bodies. But sometimes heavy periods can cause anemia (uh-NEE-mee-uh). Anemia is a disease of the blood. It can make you feel tired out all the time. If your period is super heavy and you feel tired all the time, ask your doctor to check it out.

Q **Around the middle of my cycle my vaginal discharge gets really heavy. Is it OK to use a tampon for vaginal discharge?**

A No, you should never use a tampon for vaginal discharge. Your vaginal discharge has a job to do. It helps keep your vagina clean and moist. A tampon would dry up the discharge inside your vagina, and the discharge couldn't do its job.

ten

Yours Alone

Respecting and Protecting Your Body

Puberty is a time to feel good about your body. But this isn't always easy. Sometimes other people make it hard. People may react to your changing body in ways that you don't like. Your family, friends, or other kids at school may tease you. Even strangers on the street may make comments about your body. They can make you feel bad.

Just Walk On By

Has this ever happened to you? You're walking down the street. A car full of guys drives by. You don't know them. They start to whistle or yell stuff at you, like "Oh, baby" or "Hey, hot stuff, come on over here."

You know the kind of things they say. This sort of attention can be a little scary. So how do you deal with it?

You might think of a smart comeback to yell at them. But it's best not to answer back. Who knows what kind of nuts they are? You don't want to egg them on. For sure, you don't want them to stop the car and get out. Just pretend you don't hear them. Keep on walking. Go toward other people, into a store, somewhere safe.

Doing Something

What if someone says something that really bothers or upsets you? You don't have to ignore this behavior.

"On my way to school I pass a new building that's going up. The guys who work there bug me. When they see me they whistle and say sexual things. I don't like the way that makes me feel."

In a case like this, you can do something. Talk to your parents. They can talk to the owners of the building. Or they can talk to the company the men work for. Explain what is going on. It's their job to stop it. You could even report the problem to the police.

Being Safe

Sometimes strangers can say and do things that are real scary. Don't talk with anyone that scares you. Trust your feelings. Be strong!

I was walking my dog in the park. This guy came up and started asking questions. How big were my breasts? Did I have my period yet? I acted like I was racing my dog. "Come on, Rusty, let's go race." And I ran home.

This girl did the smart thing. She acted quickly and got away from that person.

My mom was shopping. I was waiting for her in the car. A man comes over and sort of leans into the car. He's saying this creepy stuff, coming on to me. I shouted at him, loud enough so other people could hear. "I'm only ten years old. Get out of here!" I was really yelling loud, and he left. Then my mom came back, and I told her all about it.

This girl did the smart thing, too. She acted quickly. In clear and loud words she told the creep to go away. People like this don't want others to see what they're doing.

If anything like this happens to you, get out of harm's way. Run away if you have to. Run

Some Good Advice:

Don't think it's all in your head.

Don't think you're being "too sensitive."

If it makes you feel bad, it should be stopped.

Don't accept excuses like:

"Boys will be boys."

"Everybody does it."

"It's always been that way."

toward other people. Shout or yell to get other people's attention. Later, talk to an adult you trust. Talk to your mom, dad, or a teacher about what happened.

Above all, don't blame yourself. Don't feel ashamed. The person bothering you is to blame, not you.

Harassment at School

Harass means to bother. The stories above are all examples of *sexual harassment*. But it isn't always strangers who harass. Other kids at school may harass you.

Everyone has the right to feel safe and be happy at school. You have the right to learn, study, and join in school activities. And you have the right to do these things in a comfortable setting. Sexual harassment gets in the way of this right. It can make it hard to pay attention in class. Or play on a sports team. Or just walk through the halls.

Dealing with Harassment at School

Too often we are told to "just ignore it" when other kids harass us. Maybe this advice works in some cases. But most of the time, "just ignoring it" doesn't work. Someone must face up to the harasser and tell him or her to stop.

What Exactly Is Harassment?

Harassment can be touching, pinching, or grabbing. It can be someone grabbing your breasts, private parts, or butt. It can be someone rubbing up against you. But it doesn't have to involve body contact. Here are some examples:

- **Making sexual comments about a person's body**

- **Teasing and calling names**

- **Telling "dirty" jokes or "sex" stories**

- **Making rude gestures, whistling, or catcalls**

- **Staring at your breasts or private parts**

- **Spreading sexual rumors or gossip**

- **Showing "dirty" pictures**

- **Pressuring someone for dates or kissing**

- **Threatening sexual violence**

Telling one "dirty" joke isn't harassment. Grabbing someone's breasts, even once, is. Even things like "dirty" jokes can become harassment when they happen over and over again.

There are a number of things you can do. What you do depends on the type of harassment. How often does it happen? How serious is it? Here is some advice:

Don't think it's all in your head. Don't think you're being "too sensitive." If it makes you feel bad, it should be stopped.

Keep track of what happens. Keep a diary. Each time something happens, write down the date and tell what happened. Tell who was there and where it happened. Tell a friend who can back you up.

Tell the harasser to stop. It's important to let him, or her, know that their actions upset you. Be real clear about what's bothering you.

Get a parent, teacher, or school counselor to help you. The harasser may be more likely to listen to an adult. It takes a lot of courage to stop the harassment. Ask a friend or an adult to support you.

Don't accept excuses like: "Boys will be boys." "Everybody does it." "It's always been that way."

Report the problem to your principal.

Sexual harassment at school is illegal! Schools have to take action if a student is being harassed. Usually it can be stopped without having to take legal action. But if the harassment doesn't stop, you can consider it.

Sexual harassment is not like homework, zits, and tests. It's not something you have to put up with.

Know your rights. Sexual harassment is not like homework, zits, and tests. It's not something you have to put up with.

Abuse

Your body belongs to you. No one is allowed to touch you in a sexual way. It doesn't matter if that person is a parent, a relative, a friend, minister, rabbi, priest, or a stranger. They shouldn't touch you in a way that doesn't feel right to you. You and you alone decide what feels right. Trust yourself! Trust your feelings!

Trust yourself!

Trust your feelings!

If someone has touched you in this way, don't keep it a secret. No matter what it is, *you haven't done anything wrong*. You're the kid. No matter what anyone might say, *it's not your fault*. No matter what anyone might say, *you don't have to protect the person that does this to you*. Talk to an adult you trust. Tell them the whole story. Let them help you.

Abuse Hotline

There is a hotline set up to help young people deal with abuse. (The abuse can be sexual, physical, or emotional.) This hotline lets you talk to a trained person. You don't have to give them your name, and it doesn't cost any money. It's called the National Child Abuse Hotline. The number is **1-800-422-4453 (1-800-4-A-CHILD)**.

As we've seen, puberty is a time of change. Your body changes. Your feelings change. But the changes all fit together. And you grow from a child to a woman.

During puberty, you are becoming your own self. You get treated with respect. You treat others with respect. You have more responsibility. You learn you have a right to your own feelings and thoughts.

We hope this book has helped you. Helped you to know how your body changes. Helped you to explore your own feelings. Helped you to cope with the difficulties of growing up.

But no book is perfect. You may still want to know more. You may still have questions you want answered.

So talk to people about puberty. Ask questions. Ask your parents and teachers. Ask your grandmother and other relatives. Don't be shy. Go to the library and look for other books on puberty. Find out as much as you can about this very special time in your life. And, enjoy growing up.

P.P.S. Just in case you read the introduction and want to know about my granddaughter: Olivia is here! My daughter, Area, gave birth just as I was finishing this book. Olivia weighed nine pounds, three ounces. I was there in the delivery room when Olivia came out of my daughter's body. It was amazing. She is amazing. Life is amazing. Remember that.

Index

A
abuse, 120-21
anemia, 114
anorexia, 61
anus, 77, 79
areola, 21

B
baby, growth of, 84-85, 89-90
benzoyl peroxide, 67-68, 70
body hair. *See* hair
body odor (b.o.), 63, 64-65, 70
  sex organs, odor of, 78, 79-80
  telling friend about, 70
bras, 24-29
  choices of, 27-28
  first bra, 24-26
  measuring for, 26-27
  sizes of, 26-27
breasts, 19
  areola, 21
  beginning of, 20-21, 30
  bras, sizes and types of, 24-29
  buds, 20-21, 22, 30, 97
  nipples, 21, 22-23, 39
  periods and, 97
  pubic hair growth and, 33, 35
  questions and answers about, 29-30
  size and shape of, 23-24, 29-30
  soreness, 20
  stages of development, 21-23
  teasing from others about, 30
  TV breasts, 23-24
bulimia, 61-62

C
caffeine, 111
calcium needs, 46-47, 49, 57
cervix, 83-85
clitoris, 73, 74-75
coffee or tea, 49
cramps, 109-10
cravings for food, 110

D
deodorant, 65, 70, 79
dieting, 52-54. *See also* nutrition

E
eating disorders, 55, 61-62
exercise, 58-59, 111

F
facial hair, 40
feet, growth of, 43, 44

G
greasy hair, 65
growth patterns. *See also* height spurt; weight spurt
  calcium needs, 46-47, 49
  coffee or tea, effects of, 49
  feet, 43, 44
  growing pains, 48
  growing up in puberty, 17-18
  height. *See* height spurt
  periods, onset of, 48
  shortness, 45, 46, 49
  smoking, effects of, 49-50
  stunting growth, 49-50
  weight. *See* weight spurt

H
hair
  facial hair, 40
  moustache (upper lip), 40
  nipple hair, 39
  oily hair, 65
  pubic hair, 32-35, 38-39, 73, 98
  shaving legs and underarms, 35-37, 39
  underarm and body hair, 35-37, 39
  waxing removal of, 40
harassment, 116-20
height spurt, 42-43. *See also* growth patterns
  boys, taller than, 42-43, 44
  calcium needs, 46-47, 49
  clues to height, 45-46
  feet growth, 43, 44
  growing pains, 48
  periods, onset of, 48
  scoliosis, 48-49
  shortness, 45, 46, 49
  stunting growth, 49-50
hymen, 76-77, 78, 112

M
masturbation, 80
medication
  cramps, for, 110
  pimples, for, 67-69, 70
menstruation. *See* period
mons, 72, 73
moustache, 40

N
National Child Abuse Hotline, 121
nipples, 21, 22-23

hair on, 39
nutrition
  breakfast, importance of, 57
  calcium needs, 46-47, 49, 57
  dieting, 52-54
  junk food, 56-57
  PMS (premenstrual syndrome), help for, 111
  serving, definition of, 59
  water, 56
  weight worries and, 56-58

O
odor. *See* body odor (b.o.)
oily hair, 65
orgasm, 80
ova (eggs), 83, 89-91
ovaries, 83, 84
ovulation, 89-91

P
parents
  first bra, 25-26
  talking to parents about periods and puberty, 100-102
period
  amount of blood, 87-89, 93-94
  anemia, chance of, 114
  bleeding between periods, 93-94
  celebration of, 101-2
  cramps, 109-10
  early and late first periods, 112-13
  emotions during, 110
  first period, 48, 95-102

Readers Love Lynda Madaras

"I am ten years old and read your book a little each day, and I love it. I think this is a great book and it will help a lot of people."
— Jennifer, age 10

"I wanted you to know I loved your book *My Body, My Self*. It made me feel special."
— Marika, age 11

"My daughter and I have spent many hours going through The *"What's Happening to My Body?" Book for Girls* and discussing many topics....Thank you for writing a wonderful book."
— Leigh, mother of a 9-year-old

"I've read your book The *"What's Happening to My Body?" Book for Boys* twice already. I always found it hard talking to somebody about this subject. Your book really helped me understand and clear things up a little."
— Bryan, age 14

"Your book is just fantastic, absolutely excellent...I can't believe you, a mom, knew this stuff."
— Pat, age 12

Lynda Madaras is the author of 12 books on health, childcare, and parenting, including three American Library Association "Best Book of the Year" award winners. She is recognized worldwide by librarians, teachers, parents, nurses, doctors, and especially kids for her unique, non-threatening style, excellent organization, and thorough coverage of the experience of adolescence. For more than 20 years a sex and health education teacher for girls and boys in California, she conducts workshops for teachers, parents, and librarians, and has appeared on *Oprah*, CNN, PBS, and *Today*. She lectures frequently to teachers, librarians, nurses, and parents about talking about puberty with children.

The "What's Happening to My Body?" Series

THE "WHAT'S HAPPENING TO MY BODY?" BOOK FOR GIRLS, 3RD EDITION
A Growing-Up Guide for Preteens and Teens
Lynda Madaras with Area Madaras

This classic book covers the body's changing size and shape, breasts, the reproductive organs, the menstrual cycle, pubic hair, puberty in boys, diet, exercise, health, and much more.

304 pages. 5¼" x 8". 51 black-and-white drawings.

MY BODY, MY SELF FOR GIRLS, 2ND EDITION
Lynda Madaras & Area Madaras

The companion workbook to *The "What's Happening to My Body?" Book for Girls.*

Illustrated with drawings, cartoons, and photos, here are stories, quizzes, exercises, checklists, illustrations, and lots of personal anecdotes about body image, diet, height, weight, pimples, cramps, first periods, first bras, and first impressions.

128 pages. 7¼" x 9". Over 40 drawings.

MY FEELINGS, MY SELF, 2ND EDITION
A Growing-Up Guide for Girls
Lynda Madaras & Area Madaras

So that a young girl can explore her thoughts and feelings about herself, her parents, and her friends, this popular workbook/journal provides answers, along with stories and letters from teens and preteens expressing their feelings about what's going on in their lives.

160 Pages. 7¼" x 9". 30 drawings. Bibliography

READY, SET, GROW!
A "What's Happening to My Body?" Book for Younger Girls
Lynda Madaras

Written especially for 8–11-year-old girls and playfully illustrated with lively cartoon drawings, *Ready, Set, Grow!* covers all of the new and exciting changes girls can expect.

128 pages. 7" x 7". Over 60 2-color illustrations.

THE "WHAT'S HAPPENING TO MY BODY?" BOOK FOR BOYS, 3RD EDITION
A Growing-Up Guide for Preteens and Teens
Lynda Madaras with Area Madaras

The classic puberty education book for boys covers the body's changing size and shape, hair, voice changes, perspiration, pimples, the reproductive organs, sexuality, puberty in girls, and much more.

288 pages. 5¼" x 8". 48 black-and-white drawings.

MY BODY, MY SELF FOR BOYS, 2ND ÉDITION
Lynda Madaras & Area Madaras

The companion workbook to *The "What's Happening to My Body?" Book for Boys.*

Packed with drawings, cartoons, games, checklists, quizzes, and innovative exercises, this helpful workbook includes special sections on the body, body image, height, weight, growing size and shape, hair, voice changes, reproductive organs, and sexuality.

112 pages. 7¼" x 9". Over 60 drawings & photos.

See the next page for order form.

LYNDA AND AREA MADARAS BOOKS FOR PRETEENS AND TEENS (AND THEIR FAMILIES, FRIENDS, AND TEACHERS)

Order from your local bookstore, or write or call: Newmarket Press, 18 East 48th Street, New York, NY 10017; (212) 832-3575 or (800) 669-3903; Fax (212) 832-3629; E-mail sales@newmarketpress.com

Please send me the following books by Lynda Madaras:

THE "WHAT'S HAPPENING TO MY BODY?" BOOK FOR GIRLS
_____ copies at $22.95 each (gift hardcover)
_____ copies at $12.95 each (trade paperback)

MY BODY, MY SELF FOR GIRLS
_____ copies at $12.95 each (trade paperback)

MY FEELINGS, MY SELF
A Growing-Up Guide For Girls
_____ copies at $12.95 each (trade paperback)

READY, SET, GROW!
A "What's Happening to My Body?" Book for Younger Girls
_____ copies at $22.00 each (gift hardcover)
_____ copies at $12.00 each (trade paperback)

THE "WHAT'S HAPPENING TO MY BODY?" BOOK FOR BOYS
_____ copies at $22.95 each (gift hardcover)
_____ copies at $12.95 each (trade paperback)

MY BODY, MY SELF FOR BOYS
_____ copies at $12.95 each (trade paperback)

For postage and handling, add $4.00 for the first book, plus $1.00 for each additional book. New York residents please add applicable sales tax. Please allow 4-6 weeks for delivery. Prices and availability subject to change.

I enclose a check or money order, payable to Newmarket Press, in the amount of $_____.

Name _____

Address _____

_____

City/State/Zip _____

Special discounts are available for orders of five or more copies. For information, contact Newmarket Press, Special Sales Dept., 18 East 48th Street, New York, NY 10017; (212) 832-3575 or (800) 669-3903; Fax (212) 832-3629; E-mail sales@newmarketpress.com   **www.newmarketpress.com**